THE liminal CHRYSALIS

Imagining Reproduction and Parenting Futures Beyond the Binary

T0294167

Edited by Kori Doty and A.J. Lowik

DEMETER

The Liminal Chrysalis
Imagining Reproduction and Parenting Futures Beyond the Binary
Edited By Kori Doty and A.J. Lowik

Demeter Press
2546 10th Line
Bradford, Ontario
Canada, L3Z 3L3
Tel: 289-383-0134
Email: info@demeterpress.org
Website: www.demeterpress.org

Demeter Press logo based on the sculpture "Demeter" by Maria-Luise Bodirsky www.keramik-atelier.bodirsky.de

Printed and Bound in Canada

Front cover: Michelle Lee, Broadview Design
Typesetting: Michelle Pirovich
Proof reading: Jena Woodhouse

Library and Archives Canada Cataloguing in Publication
Title: The liminal chrysalis: imagining reproduction and parenting futures beyond the binary / edited by H. Kori Doty and A.J. Lowik.
Names: Doty, H. Kori, editor. | Lowik, A.J., editor.
Description: Includes bibliographical references.
Identifiers: Canadiana 20210364912 | ISBN 9781772583588 (softcover)
Subjects: LCSH: Transgender parents. | LCSH: Gender nonconformity. | LCSH: Parenting. | LCSH: Feminism. | LCSH: Human reproduction.
Classification: LCC HQ77.93. L56 2022 | DDC 306.874086/7—dc23

To Searyl, for making me a seahorse papa. To Sharon, Kristine, Verna, and the countless gestators before them who played a part in my lineage. And to those who have become family beyond blood and bone in all the queerest ways: Coco, Katie, Maxwell, Beckham, Serena, barbara, Gavin, Johan, Fern, and all of all y'alls children.

—Kori Doty

To my parents, Barbara and Marvin Lowik, who have loved and supported me through numerous coming-outs. To Steven, my brother, who switched to calling me his sib with ease and enthusiasm. To Graeme, my brother, who protected me from high school bullies and introduced me to queer music. I am thriving as a non-binary adult because of you. It is a gift, in a world that can't and won't make sense of who I am, to know that you are in my corner, always.

—A.J. Lowik

Acknowledgments

Thank you to Dr. Andrea O'Reilly and everyone at Demeter Press for believing in this collection from start to finish. It feels momentous for a feminist motherhood press to take on a book about challenging binaries in reproductive and parenting worlds—motherhood/fatherhood among them.

If it were not for the support of Julia Lane, this book would not have been possible. Thank you, Julia, for your enthusiasm for this project from the very beginning and for always being available to help talk us through the ins and outs of the process. As first-time editors, we are so grateful for your guidance.

To the three anonymous peer reviewers who read an earlier version of this collection and provided thoughtful, thorough, and passionate feedback, thank you. This book has become a stronger, more inclusive piece of work thanks to you.

Preamble

The world in which these chapters were written and gathered no longer exists. As we completed a round of edits on the collection and began to draft the introduction, the world found itself in a crisis state as a result of the COVID-19 pandemic. The pieces in this collection were all written before this virus, which has had such a dramatic influence on medical and educational systems, civic society, parenting practices, and families across the world. The authors share stories about engaging with systems and structures that are now radically changing in the face of this pandemic. The climate in which these authors were making gendered, reproductive, and parenting (as well as research) decisions is now substantially, perhaps irreversibly, changed. We do not know if or when things will go back to normal (not that the previous system was working in ways that we would like to return to), nor do we know what the world will look like on the other side of this global transition. We are living in the liminal space of this pandemic. We will never return to the time of before, and there are so many uncertainties about what will come after. In this moment of now, we, the editors of this collection, had planned to write the introduction to this collection sitting side by side, feeding off each other's ideas and energies, writing each new sentence collaboratively, together. Instead, we share a Google document where we write sections as disconnected fragments, send each other e-mail updates, and connect over Zoom for short spurts, when Kori's kid is in bed for the night, after long and exhausting days of just getting by. But we remain committed to seeing this collection come to fruition, a tangible object you can hold in our hand, so we trudge on and count ourselves lucky for having been entrusted with the stories found here.

We offer this collection as an archival glimpse into genders, families, practices, knowledge, and systems that may never be the same again.

As physical distancing and quarantine protocols are catalyzing massive shifts in social society, books like this one, records of our stories, are even more important than ever. Queer and trans people—and most notably queer and trans people negotiating reproductive, parenting and family life—were already isolated and marginalized. Many of the authors in the collection share their experiences of this isolation and marginalization, both in terms of their personal lives and due to rarely seeing their lives reflected in academic writing and popular culture alike. We know that this pandemic is only exasperating that isolation and marginalization. We see inequities intensifying and power imbalances proliferating. We see parents struggling to do it all. If it takes a village, what happens to marginalized people when their village has to stay away? Within the pages of this collection, you will read about non-binary and other variously located people who have been forced to chart a path for themselves on a terrain that was not built with their lives and needs in mind. You will read about marginalized knowledges, which have been suppressed and rejected and are now being reclaimed. Within these pages, you will read research and commentaries and stories that challenge Western binaries in many forms—chapters which expose the injustices of the "before," which offer hope for the "after." The authors of the chapters contained here are leaders from whom we can learn so much, especially now. They reclaim ancestral knowledge and traditions, navigate cisrepronormative biological imperatives, push against cultural norms and critiques, foster healing and hope, all in an effort to survive and thrive in their own ways, on their own terms. We can all learn from their resistance and resilience.

A.J. and Kori

Contents

Introduction

A.J. Lowik and Kori Doty

Binary oppositions abound in Western contemporary language and thought. The relationship between these pairs of linguistic terms is typically hierarchical, where one half of the pair dominates or is privileged over the other and where the subordinate term often represents an absence of or lack of the first. From good-evil to mind-body and culture-nature, these binary oppositions inform Western philosophical and political values, creating boundaries and borders between this and that—where power informs not only where the boundary is drawn but also which of the pair is understood as superior to the other. Reproduction and parenting norms and narratives are no exception, as they are laden with oppositional pairs that create limits on how we can think, act, and identify and on which we create meaning and pass judgement. For instance, Jorden Allen and Julia Moore analyze the experiences of familial estrangement to call attention to the problematic functional-dysfunctional family binary, and Nyna Amin demonstrates how within the context of poverty, the child-parent binaries are fragile categories, subject to subversion and reversal. Anna Wierzbicka identifies the religious, puritanical, and moralistic roots of the Anglo parental speech of "good boy-girl"—meant to praise children for their actions—which is contrasted with the "bad boy-girl," whose behaviour is conversely framed as reprehensible. From wanted-unwanted pregnancies to categorizations of parents as either fit or unfit, to the configuration of the "good mother" (juxtaposed against its binary opposite of the "bad mother") which has been deconstructed extensively in the literature—(Kim and Hwang; Marshall, Godfrey and Renfrew; Narcisco et al.)—there are countless binaries within the realm of parenting and reproduction that have been (or ought to be) subject to analysis.

This collection concerns itself with the identification and decon-struction of reproduction and parenting binaries that are concerned with issues of sex, gender, sexuality, and (dis)embodied reproductive experiences, ranging from menstruation to egg donation to fertility preservation technologies. We focus primarily, but not exclusively, on the binaries of sex (male-female), gender (man-woman), parenting role (father-mother), parenting relationship (parent-non-parent), as well as the cisnormative, heteronormative, repronormative and transnormative assumptions, which are built on these binary foundations and which pervasively circulate in parenting and reproductive narratives and norms. Although thinking about "beyond the binary" futures for parents and reproductive possibilities is not limited to these avenues, our own personal entanglements with these topics, as well as their having been considered only in limited ways in the existing literature, merit intentional focus.

Arguably, the socially, medically, and legally constructed binary of male-female is at the core of our analysis (Fausto-Sterling, "Gender/Sex"; Fausto-Sterling, "The Five Sexes"; Greenberg). Sex is often treat-ed as an immutable, undisputable, and biological fact, where so-called males and females are regarded as categorically distinct from one another. A complex entanglement of genetics, chromosomes, gonads, internal and external morphological factors, hormones, and phenotypic sex characteristics is often, problematically, reduced to an either/or medical and legal assignment based on the appearance of the genitals of in-utero fetuses and neonates (Fausto-Sterling, "Gender/Sex"; Fausto-Sterling, "The Five Sexes"; Greenberg). So pervasive is the ideological grip of binary sex that it finds its way into places that it arguably does not belong. Consider, for example, that despite evidence that there is significant variation in alcohol metabolism between people of the so-called same sex (Thomasson), gendered low-risk drinking guidelines exist in many places of the world, where the guidelines for men are always higher than those for women. The problematic conflation between sex and gender in these guidelines has been critiqued elsewhere (Lowik, Hoong, and Knight). Suffice to say that countless complicated matters of science (and gender) have been reduced to a matter of sex.

Beyond that, however, the existence of intersex people, whose sexed bodies do not neatly align with the categories of male or female, draws our attention to the constructed nature of this binaristic classification system. Gross injustices have been committed against intersex infants in the name of shoring up this binary, although these injustices have been met with a strong, vocal response from activists and scholars alike (Greenberg; ISNA). Controversial psychologist John Money infamously pressured anxious parents into consenting to surgical interventions; intersex births were framed as emergencies in need of an immediate medical solution (Murray). Despite his initial test cases being declared successes by his own estimation, the passage of time would prove otherwise (Colapinto). Whereas binary sex is understood as an immutable fact on the one hand, it is considered subject to change and intervention only in the case of intersex births. Despite its obvious complexity, the fact of the binary sex is violently thrown around in ways that erase the realities of intersex bodies and people and is used as evidence of the supposed impossibility of trans existence and as a justification for the refusal, by some, to refer to intersex and trans people by the correct names, pronouns, and genders.

Furthermore, binary sex differences are essentialized and naturalized due to the procreative potential resulting from the sexual union of (some) female and (some) male bodies. That is, sexual reproduction is possible when certain kinds of bodies engage in certain kinds of sex acts. Therefore, the ability of some bodies to be reproductive is taken as evidence of the fact and necessity of biological sexual dimorphism. Certain sexed bodies are framed as complementary due to their presumed ability to reproduce when they come together and engage in certain kinds of sex. Here, we see one of the major logics for the idea of compulsory heterosexuality, in which heterosexuality is understood as the natural state based on its assumed proximity to reproduction (Rich). In the cishetero-queer binary oppositional pairing, cisheterosexual relations (specifically monogamous ones) are framed as a biological predisposition and as socially desirable, especially as compared to the sexualities of gay, lesbian, bisexual, pansexual, queer, and polyamorous people which are framed as unnatural or even immoral (O'Brien). Although it is true that the ability to reproduce is a significant marker of sex, to collapse the complex human (sexed and gendered) experience to a matter of who can and cannot reproduce using those sexed bodies is a grave injustice. It renders infertile bodies—whether due to injury, contraceptive use, intersex status, radiation exposure, or surgical intervention—as somehow less male or female and by extension not proper men and women. For example, polycystic ovarian syndrome has been called "the thief of womanhood" (Kitzinger and Willmott) and failing at motherhood has been described as a threat to womanhood, insofar as cisgender women's social identities have been constructed around their reproductive capacities (Tsui and Cheng).

Repronormativity, then, is multifold. First, it refers to the ways in which female assigned bodies and women's identities, in particular, are maternalized; female/women's subjectivity is tied so intricately with reproduction that the possibilities for nonreproductive sexual desire, pleasure, and identity are foreclosed (Franke). Like heterosexuality, reproduction becomes compulsory. More specifically, repronormativity speaks to the ways in which reproduction becomes compulsory for some but prohibited for others. It is the process by which some are rendered fit and others unfit. It is the scaffolding on which other binaries of parenting and reproduction are constructed, and this scaffolding is the racist, sexist, cisheterosexist, and colonial foundation on which nations are built (Lowik, "Reproducing Eugenics"; Weissman).

In Western sociocultural, medico-legal, and political contexts, gender is itself understood as a binary. In the same way that it is assumed that there are only two "natural" sexes, it is further assumed that there are only two "natural" genders, with all their accompanying norms, roles, and stereotypes, where each gender is thought to normatively correspond to one of the two sexes. People with male assigned bodies are understood always-already as boys, men, husbands, and fathers, and people with female assigned bodies are understood as always-already girls, women, wives, and mothers. Trans and nonbinary people, of all identities and expressions, are therefore framed as the exception, even as aberrational. This cisnormativity is so pervasive and prevalent that it is not only difficult for many to recognize but also taken as another immutable truth on which we have built systems and structures, and which informs our delivery of healthcare, among other things (Bauer et al.). It is so pervasive that sex and gender are often conflated, confused, and used as interchangeable even among researchers, scholars, law- and policymakers, and statisticians, who one might assume should know better (at the risk of sounding prescriptivist). This is true of HIV research (Poteat, German, and

Flynn), of legal contexts (Valdes), of alcohol research and guidelines (Lowik, Hoong, and Knight), of studies concerned with the impact of disability on life expectancy (Snow), and beyond.

The discursively constructed positions of mother and father rely on this oppositional sex-gender binary as well. There have been many changes in how cisgender men and women parent; for example, more cis men are engaging in the acts of caring, nurturing, and affective tasks of parenthood (Nentwich). However, the expectation of mother as primary carer and father as financial provider binary remains (Nentwich), and these caring acts by fathers have been frequently classified as men performing acts of mothering. As A.J. Lowik has argued elsewhere, "the binary, gendered and role-based foundations of parenting discourse is, at best, minimally challenged when this nurturing is labelled as 'motherly'" ("The Ties That Bind" 213); they later continue:

> When maternal practice is understood as having gender flexibility, this is nevertheless a cis-focused flexibility, where male experiential knowledge is reduced to include only these experiences of cisgender men. It is also problematic to frame all acts of parenting as either acts of mothering or fathering; this binary approach to parenting discourse does not reflect the queer ways in which trans* people parent, from the names they choose to be called by their kids to the ways they ungender the embodied aspects of parenting, like breastfeeding... cisgender men who identify as fathers and engage in the *mush* of parenting are essentially muted when these behaviours are framed as "acts of mothering." ("The Ties That Bind" 216-217)

The challenging of trans people's gender identities based on their reproductive and parenting practices is arguably a result of trans-normativity, which is a set of binary and medicalized standards against which we hold trans people accountable (Johnson; Lowik, "Betwixt, Between, Besides"). That is, when trans people are considered, two further assumptions are made. First, it is assumed that trans folks fall into two binary gender categories (i.e., trans women and trans men), arguably a carryover from the pervasive, essentialized two sex-gender binary. This is not to say that trans men and women are not "real", are gender dupes, or any of the other highly prejudicial ways that trans people have been painted by so-called feminists of the past and present (who we intentionally do not cite here, as an act of resistance). Rather, we mean only to acknowledge that the sex-gender binary system has undoubtedly affected how binary trans people have been able to imagine, experience, and construct their identities as well as make sense of their relationship to their bodies. Cisgender identities and embodiments have too been similarly restrained and restricted in binaristic ways because of this pervasive dualism. The second transnormative assumption is that trans people will engage, or at least ought to desire engagement, with medical transition options to align their sexed bodies with their gender identities (Johnson; Lowik, "Betwixt, Between, Besides"). Cisnormativity is at work here, too— it is as if cisgender sex-gender alignment is the only and the correct way to be gendered. The dominant narrative of "the wrong body" (in which a trans man is understood as a man trapped in a woman's body, or vice versa) reifies this cisnormative relationship between the sexed body and gendered personhood. Again, this is not to suggest that trans people for whom this narrative rings true should be denied the gender-affirming medical transition that they require. Rather, we argue, as others have before us, that the idea of a wrong body prompts critical reflection on its binary opposite; if there is a wrong body, there is implicitly, conversely, a right body, which is the cisgender body (Hughes). Cisgender relationships between sex and gender are essentialized and unquestioned in their hierarchical position within this binary pairing, whereas trans relationships between sex and gender are scrutinized and are deemed wrong unless medically corrected. Taken together, transnormative assumptions render invisible the plethora of non-binary and nonmedicalized experiences of trans identity and expression.

Transnormativity is further tied together with reproductive experiences and parenting possibilities. Consider that losing reproductive capacities is framed as the small price to pay for medical transition (T'Sjoen, Van Caenegem, and Wierckx). This price is paid largely by trans folks who have been ill-informed about the fertility-related consequences of their gender-affirming transitions, who have been unable to pay the hefty price of fertility-preservation technologies, and for whom access to gender-affirming medical transition is an urgent and dire matter, making the difference between life and death.

Consider also that along with the wrong body trope come numerous prescriptions about who counts as truly trans. Sexual reproduction and parenthood, in this framing, are viewed as antithetical to transness, in much the same way that, generations ago, identifying as gay or lesbian was understood as antithetical to parenthood, to family, to the nation, and to the future of humanity itself (Edelman). For instance, the 1995 New Zealand case of *Attorney General v. Otahuhu Family Court* held that a postoperative transsexual person could only marry someone of the now 'opposite sex' if they "no longer operate in his or her original sex" (Cruz 1168-69). That is, a (trans) man who was assigned female at birth could be legally recognized as a man and eligible to marry a woman if he "never appear[ed] unclothed as a woman, or enter[ed] into a sexual relationship as a woman, or procreate[d]" (Cruz 1168-69). One study found that for trans men who did experience pregnancy, "the negative attitude of both therapists and medical professionals that pregnancy and birth represented a contraindication of the diagnosis of transsexuality proved to be one of the most prominent stress factors during pregnancy" (More 325). In the 2002 case *Re: Gardiner Estate* in the United States, the state found that the litigant, a trans woman, was not a woman for the purposes of marriage because "a male-to-female post-operative transsexual does not fit the definition of a female. The male organs have been removed, but the ability to 'produce ova and bear offspring' does not and never did exist" (Karaian 218). The courts relied on a dictionary definition of sex that focuses on reproductive abilities to determine that the litigant was not legally a woman, so her marriage had never been legally valid; as a result, her petition to receive her deceased husband's death benefits was denied. More than being unable to reproduce according to her male sex assignment, the courts required that the litigant be able to reproduce according to her gender identity in order to be recognized as a woman for the purposes of marriage and for it to have always been so ("does not and never did exist"). Of course, many responded to this legal decision by pointing out that this logic disqualifies prepubescent girls, post-menopausal women, and any woman with fertility problems from the category of woman (Karaian). Nevertheless, *Re: Gardiner Estate* demonstrates how repronormativity is interconnected with legal gendered personhood. More than requiring the physical erasure of one gender to take on another, some courts have denied trans people legal recognition on the basis of their inability to reproduce according to their gender identity, despite the obvious flaws in this logic.

Another aspect of transnormativity is arguably that one ought to desire congruence between gender identity, reproductive ability, and parenting role. A trans woman, as a woman, it is reasoned, will/should ultimately yearn for the reproductive capacities associated with cisgender women, namely gestational motherhood; a trans man, as a man, it is reasoned, will/should ultimately reject a gestational role as demonstrative of his man-ness (More; Doussa). Transnormativity requires that one completely erase and reject the roles, norms, as well as the reproductive and parenting experiences cisnormatively associated with their sex assigned body in favour of those associated with their gender, thus shoring up the cisnormative sex-gender binary. There is no room for non-binary people, let alone beyond the binary reproductive and parenting practices, which are increasingly being taken up by binary and non-binary trans folks and cisgender people alike.

It is within this complicated landscape of binaries that we situate this collection—as a challenge to the constructedness of sex, on which the gender binary is built; as a challenge to the constructedness of compulsory heterosexuality, which is itself reliant on the sex-gender binaries; as a challenge to the transnormative assumptions which limit trans reproductive and parenting possibilities; as a challenge to the repronormative way that sexed bodies are affixed to gender identities, which are tethered to reproductive experiences, which are tied to parenting roles, all in the service of fit parents being put to work building nation-states. We imagine a future for reproduction and parenting beyond the binary. This entire collection is a liminal chrysalis.

We cherish the magical, ambiguous, and disorientating space of the in between and the beyond, drawing on Victor Turner's liminality for the title of this collection. Turner's original use of the concept of liminality was mobilized within the context of cultural rites of passage and transition rituals. For instance, marriage rituals may require that one cross a threshold (jumping over a broom, stepping across a doorway); at graduation, one crosses a stage; upon entry into the army or adulthood, or following a death, one cuts one's hair. There is a moment, a phase when one is neither here nor there, neither this nor that, but in a transitory, precarious, ambiguous, and even dangerously unstable state of in between. For Turner, it was in that liminal phase that magical transformation occurs. If a person was unmarried on this side of the doorway and married on the other, then the threshold between this room and that room is where the transition between states of being happens. In rites of passage, the time spent in this liminal space is fleeting—one (relatively) quickly passes from here to there and becomes a new thing on the other side. Liminality has also been deployed to conceptualize reproductive and parenthood experiences, such as Gill Watson's work that explores the crisis, uncertainty, and powerlessness of parents with preterm infants or work that frames infertility, pregnancy, birth, nursing, and miscarriage as liminal dimensions or experiences (Allan; Dowling and Pontin; Reiheld). We are inspired by these deployments of liminality, as well by both Turner and social anthropologist Mary Douglas, when we think about liminality as more than a transitional and temporary state. There are liminal personas or beings, who are not categorizable as one thing or another; they find the ambiguous, in between space and stay there. In fantasy, mythology, and folklore, there are hybrid beings like centaurs and satyrs, ghosts who are neither dead nor alive, and science fiction cyborgs who are part human and part machine. There are, however, liminal beings who exist outside of the realm of fiction. We are by no means the first to consider intersex, trans, and non-binary people as liminal beings—positions that are at once powerful and unintelligible within cultures characterized by cisnormative binaries where transitional crossings are disruptive if not altogether unthinkable (Dentice and Dietert; Robertson; Wilson). Although not all authors in this collection are trans, many are; and among all authors, regardless of their gender identities, we see liminality as an evocative concept that draws attention to the power, potential, and risk of moving beyond binaries ranging from those associated with sex and gender to those associated with parenting labels, norms, and expectations. We are reminded of Leslie Feinberg's seminal work *Transgender Warriors*, wherein a bearded woman, performance artist, and juggler named Jennifer Miller reflects: "My beard is a lifelong performance. I live in a very liminal place. 'Liminal' means an 'in-between place.' It means in a doorway, a dawn or a dusk. It's a lovely place. In the theatre, it's when the lights go out. And before the performance begins" (143).

We tether liminality to the visual imagery of a chrysalis, a metaphor for a transitional state of becoming. Indeed, the butterfly is a symbol often associated with trans people due to its invocation of meta-morphosis. A chrysalis, however, is not only the liminal space between caterpillar and butterfly where a transformation occurs. We understand this phase as about a complete deconstruction of the previous state, a disintegration into primordial goo, wherein something brand new can emerge. We imagine the chapters in this collection as transformative and as offering opportunities for renewal and reconceptualization, as a primordial goo that offers insights into this state of undoing, unlearning, and unbeing. We understand the authors of those chapters, too, as being in perpetual states of becoming—who they were when they drafted these chapters has changed dramatically in the time since they were written—with months and a global pandemic wedged between their original conceptualization and this publication. Although this collection seems to fix these authors and their stories into a time and place, freezing their development, we encourage the reader to consider these chapters as a snapshot, a peek into a moment of the authors' lives—lives that have undoubtedly continued to change by the time these words meet your eyes or ears. The chapters are also disparate in their states of completeness, at least according to academic publishing standards. Whereas some of the more scholarly contributions appear polished, others are raw and fragmented. We have resisted the urge to strip these later chapters of their chrysalis quality—to render them artificially complete by a set of standards that do not reflect the lives and social locations of the authors who wrote them. With great intention, we mean to expose the powerful and risky spaces that these authors occupy and lay bare the possibilities and potential that exist within liminal, chrysalis-like spaces. Maybe in *our* disorientation, maybe in *your* disorientation in reading this collection, we can find something new.

Our goal was to create a collection that included both scholarly writing in the form of research results and critical theory as well as poetry, fiction, and firsthand accounts told by authors who had stories to share but no affiliation to academic or research institutions. We worked alongside the authors who had no previous experience navigating the MLA citation style guide or writing for a largely academic audience, and we moulded and revised their submissions with what we hope were thoughtful and sensitive suggestions, which did not compromise their voice or vision. Ultimately, we see the incredible scholarly value of stories told firsthand by so-called lay people, which are typically reduced to the realm of the anecdotal. Yet we are also committed to ensuring that the more academically oriented chapters have been written in such a way that they are accessible to people outside of academia. We include a glossary at the end of the collection, where we define some of the more complex terms that pop up within this introduction and the chapters. Furthermore, we recognize that the academic v. firsthand experiential divide is yet another reductive binary. Kamee Abrahamian's "Motherhood as Speculative (Non) Fiction" and Jan Estrellado and Alanna Aiko Moore's "Towards a Queer and Trans Model for Families of Colour," for example, bridge that binary divide; each has elegantly woven these two kinds of writing and thinking together. Olivia Fischer's master's research on non-binary people's reproductive lives coincided with and spark their own exploration of gender, and Milo Chesnut's dissertation research on gender-open parenting informs their reflection on their own childhood being raised by a feminist mother. Taq Kaur Bhandal's "Bloody Cycles" is intentionally disruptive of the hierarchy of knowledge that privileges the systematic review over ancestral knowledge and oral histories; Bhandal also elects to format her chapter in a way that will be intelligible to scholarly readers. These chapters disrupt even our own preconceived, binary categorization of the kinds of content we imagined possible for this collection, and to these authors, we are eternally grateful.

In selecting contributions for the collection, we privileged submissions where the authors were themselves members of the communities they wrote about. Recognizing that historically and today, marginalized people and knowledges have been and continue to be written about by people who exist outside of those communities and traditions, we elected to say, "No, thank you," for example, to cis-gender authors who proposed chapters where they were taking the trans pregnant body as an object of critical inquiry, and "Yes, please," to trans people who wanted to tell us about their own experience of pregnancy. Our initial call included suggested content that broadened our "beyond the binary" frame to topics falling outside of non-binary people's experiences with reproductive and parenting life, recognizing that the binaries of unwanted-wanted pregnancies, fit-unfit parents, and romantic-aromantic relationships were also worthy and relevant topics. Although we only received a few submissions that took up this understanding of beyond the binary, we see Kori Doty's interview with Pidgeon Pagonis, Estrellado and Moore's "Towards a Queer and Trans Model for Families of Colour," and Bhandal's "Bloody Cycle" as exemplary of the kind of expansive thinking that has undoubtedly pushed this collection to a place where beyond the binary thinking is much more wide-ranging that it would otherwise have been.

We have endeavoured to include contributions by a diversity of authors, including authors of colour, trans folks who were assigned male at birth, disabled authors, as well as authors from across the world. We recognize that our efforts to decentre whiteness, in particular, were not entirely successful. After our initial call for sub-missions, a thoughtful reviewer pointed out that our acknowledging the relative homogeneity of voice within the collection was not the same as taking responsibility for, changing, or challenging it. We ultimately solicited additional chapters by racialized and assigned male at birth authors. Although we feel that the collection is more balanced now, we also recognize that despite these efforts, the collection includes many contributions from white, assigned female at birth non-binary people. We recognize that our own positionalities as white, assigned female at birth non-binary editors—one of whom is affiliated with academic and research institutions—who are editing a collection for a scholarly feminist press, has undoubtedly affected who has elected to trust their stories to us. We will ensure that our future work in this area continues to push back against this homogeneity of voice, even more so than we have been able to achieve within this collection.

We begin with Chesnut's "Reflections on a Feminist Childhood from a Non-Binary Adult," a deeply personal consideration of both the strengths and shortcomings of a 1970s-1980s feminist ethic of gender-neutral (or nonsexist) childrearing. Chesnut exposes the cisnormative assumptions and expectations that were embedded in this parenting practice. Whereas children reared in this way were encouraged to explore interests, dress, and modes of being that challenged the pervasive sexism of the day, it was nevertheless assumed that each would still grow from girl to woman, from boy to man. Chesnut reminds us that even well-meaning, feminist parents may reify cisnormativity in their nonsexist approaches to childrearing. Chesnut grew into a non-binary, queer adult, a future that was unimagined/

unimaginable even as they were being raised in a way that pushed against the conventional gender socialization of the early 1980s. Working on a PhD focused on exploring the alternative parenting movements of gender-open, gender-creative, and gender-independent "theyby" parents, Chesnut reminds us that the landscape of gendered childrearing is everchanging, where non-binary parents and others actively challenge both the practices of assigning sex at birth and the nonconsensual gendering of fetuses as well as children of all ages.

"Baby Triptych" is a collection of three poems by Eitan Codish, who had originally (optimistically) envisioned writing a series of six poems, written monthly during the first six months of his child's life. The series was originally conceived as being about the adventures and challenges of raising a child without assigning them a gender. However, as you will read, Codish reflects instead on how this decision and detail took a backseat when the other challenges of childrearing became the focus of his parenting. Codish's poems are rich with diverse formatting and rely on the subtle use of gender neutral language for both his child and the reader. "Baby Triptych" reminds us of all the competing priorities and challenges of parenting, where parenting is as much a creative, improvised process as the writing of poetry.

Abrahamian's "Motherhood Is Speculative (Non)Fiction" is another experiment in writing-about-parenting-while-parenting—a chapter conceived during naptimes and written in fragments. Abrahamian plays with temporal conventions, fluctuating between the theoretical and the personal, reminding us of their entanglement, where the author's approach to parenting has been informed by the critical thinkers that they hold dear. Identifying as a queer, feminist, gender-queer, and diasporic-SWANA mother, Abrahamian explores how their gender came to be by way of their becoming a parent. They see the queering of motherhood, identifying as both genderqueer and a mother, as an act of resistance, challenging the colonial gendered conventions that tether motherhood to women.

Viridian Fen's "Parenting (Selves)" is one long poem, broken into thirty-five numbered stanzas. Within the poem, Fen reflects on the alien experience of pregnancy, where getting further along in their pregnancy increased their feelings of embodied dysphoria and discomfort and where their previously reliable techniques of bodily disconnection became increasingly challenging. After the birth, Fen actively decided to parent both their child and themself. They learned to parent their own non-binary gender into becoming while parenting their child in an atmosphere of expansive gendered possibilities. Fen reflects on the gender binaries embedded in their religious upbringing, the role technology played in their discovering the language to describe their gendered experience, and the devastation of having so few role models. Fen ends with "I teach my child what it is to be alien... My child teaches me what it is to be human"; despite the dysphoria they felt before and during their pregnancy, the child that they brought into the world was ultimately instrumental to their healing.

Serena Lukas Bhandar's "Otherhood" is a short piece of poetic prose that tells the story of her reproductive decision making as a trans femme. Bhandar describes how she accessed testosterone blockers, did not access fertility preservation technologies, and was ultimately told by her surgeon that her new vagina would be "solely for sex" and would provide "no reproductive capacity." With the conviction that not having children was the most socially responsible thing to do, and in a cloud of shame at the prospect of passing on her depression, Bhandar describes having convinced herself that childlessness was the best decision for her life. At the same time, there is tension in Bhandar's writing, where she grapples with what it would look like to have a child come into her life even without her body being a part of that process. "Otherhood" is a critical interrogation into being childless by choice, where that choice is constrained by social, personal, and medical factors. Bhandar puts her own negotiation of reproductive decision making into the broader context of trans women and trans femmes being denied access to adoption and negotiating transition after having already had children.

Artist Sunny Nestler's "The Work of Assisted Reproductive Technology in the Age of Mechanical Reproduction" is a creative chapter exploring the author's experience as a non-binary queer person who has been the genetic contributor, via egg donation, to three children (that they know of). They liken the experience to that of a sea turtle, who lays eggs which hatch into someone who the sea turtle never meets. Nestler's story untethers reproduction from parenting and contributes an often overlooked third party reproductive voice, laden with contractual obligations, a regimen of hormone therapy, and cisnormative assumptions about the gender of the donor. Indeed, the very telling of this story required careful navigation by Nestler, who acknowledges that the story was at once theirs and not theirs to tell— they thoughtfully navigate that tension in order to ensure that their story is told without compromising the confidentiality of the families with whom they are now connected. "The Work of Assisted Reproductive Technology in the Age of Mechanical Reproduction" prompts a critical consideration of the entanglement between DNA and genetics, reproductive experiences, and parenthood. Nestler's drawings, which accompany the text, are experimental depictions meant to mimic both genetic reproduction but also the processes of mutation.

Saige Whesch is a Queercrip, non-binary parent who has birthed and nursed their children while navigating life on the stolen Indigenous land called Australia. "Tales of My Infinite Chrysalis," from which we drew inspiration for the title of this book, is a collection of excerpts from the author's life, told in raw, visceral fragments that are rich with metaphor and a deep connection to the physical environment. Like Fen's "Parenting (Selves)," Whesch's pieces explore the act of parenting oneself and how this relates to parenting others. Whesch's tales queer temporality—they describe how while birthing, time twists in all directions. In "Tales from My Infinite Chrysalis," the story jumps from today to yesterday and back again; flashbacks to childhood memories are mixed with flashforwards to later events, which are mixed with dreams the author had during sleep and surgery. We move through time and space and follow along while Whesch explores partnering and parenting, all while navigating gender, name change, pronouns, medical transition decisions, legal gender recognition processes, and the Australian marriage equality vote. For Whesch, there is no end to metamorphosis. There is simply more change on the horizon.

In "Towards a Queer and Trans Model of Families of Colour: Intersections of Feminism, Race, Queerness, and Gender Identity," parents Jan E. Estrellado and Alanna Aiko Moore take turns narrating their personal and familial negotiations of racist, sexist, and cisheteronormative systems and structures. Their chapter evokes Black feminist scholar Kimberlé Crenshaw's theoretical framework of intersectionality, wherein systems of oppression overlap and are interdependent, where racism and cisheteronormativity do not exist in isolation, but where each works to reify the other. From Estrellado's struggle to find a parenting label that fits them, to the couple's challenge finding a school where they were not the only queer and trans parents of colour, to managing their child's desire for shiny pink and purple sneakers against the potential social consequences of his decision to wear them to school, Estrellado and Moore explore the burdens (and joys) of parenting as queer and trans people of colour in the United States.

Pidgeon Pagonis is an intersex activist, writer, filmmaker, and consultant. Along with Sean Saifa Wall and Lynnell Stephani, they cofounded the Intersex Justice Project, an organization dedicated to the rights of intersex people of colour in the United States and internationally. They fight to end the medically invasive and unnecessary procedures performed on the bodies of intersex neonates and infants. Doty sat down (virtually, due to COVID-19) with Pagonis to talk about how these procedures and surgeries are examples of reproductive injustice. In "An Interview with Pidgeon," Pagonis discusses how our fixation on the fallacy of sex as a binary has stripped intersex people of their reproductive futures while damaging their ability to feel sexual pleasure and satisfaction. Rather than having their genitals left alone, intersex people are denied access to fulfilling sexual and reproductive lives, all for the sake of shoring up the boundaries between the socially constructed sex categories of male and female.

Blas Radi and Moira Pérez's "'Bring in the Argentina Macho': Feminist Resistance to the Participation of AFAB Trans People in Sexual and Reproductive Rights Activism" takes us from the United States to Argentina. The authors explore the parliamentary debates regarding the legalization of abortion and how both the so-called pro-life initiatives and the feminist, pro-choice activist contingents focus on the rights of cisgender women, to the exclusion of assigned female at birth trans people. Radi and Pérez juxtapose Argentina's progressive Gender Identity Law against the pervasive cisnormativity that prevails in both their comprehensive sex education programming and in the debate over abortion legalization.

Olivia Fischer's "Lessons Learned from Researching Non-Binary Reproduction" takes us on a journey through their master's thesis research, in which they conducted interviews with five non-binary people about their experiences with conception, pregnancy, and birth. Their findings describe how non-binary people balance their reproductive goals against their medical transition, rely on community to combat isolation, to strategically choose when to disclose their gender identities to their care providers. Fischer also explores the impacts that transphobia, cisnormativity, and heteronormativity have had on the participants' reproductive and parenting decision making. Fischer contributes to the qualitative research on trans reproductive lives, which is arguably in its naissance. Their work addresses a gap in the available literature, where studies frequently focus exclusively or primarily on the experiences of binary trans people, namely trans men. Importantly, Fischer's research expands our understanding of non-binary people's reproductive lives, specifically.

Taq Kaur Bhandal's "Bloody Cycles: One Indian/Pakistani Feminist Perspective on Menstrual Health" explores three examples of menstrual or mahwari health wisdom that have been resisted by what she calls the colonial-capitalist-heteropatriarchal-extraction-based world. Bhandal considers Sikh-Punjabi gender equity and menstruation, Māori menstrual power, and African American conceptions of sacred blood to centre the experiences of people of colour and to challenge numerous binaries that are frequently deployed in the largely Western, racist, colonial world of menstruation health knowledge and research.

Finally, Lowik's "Case Study: Rowan's Experience Freezing Their Sperm" is a brief exploration of Rowan's experience freezing sperm prior to their initiating gender-affirming hormone replacement therapy. A participant in Lowik's PhD dissertation research, Rowan's story is shared in order to demonstrate how cisheteronormativity and transnormativity operated in the fertility clinic and how Rowan navigated these in pursuit of their desire to one day have genetically related children with their partner. Lowik's case study reminds us of how repronormative narratives typically tether sex to gender to reproductive capacity to parenting roles with a focus on those assigned female at birth and/or those who identify as women. Rowan's experience draws attention to the reproductive and parenting desires of those who were not female assigned and who do not identify with binary genders.

We invite you into the liminal chrysalis that is this collection. It is a window into the lives and research of the contributors prior to the COVID-19 pandemic. It was edited and finessed during the strange, surreal global lockdown. It is finding its way to you on what we hope will be 'the other side,' where things will have been reimagined anew. As you delve into these pages, we offer these questions. What magic occurs in the liminal, in between space? What emerges from the chrysalis after the period of transformation and renewal? We will return to these questions in the afterword and offer our insights into what possibilities we see for a beyond the binary future, having worked tirelessly on this collection for over two years, at a time that the world and our collective futures have never felt so uncertain.

Work Cited

Allan, Helen. "Experiences of Infertility: Liminality and the Role of the Fertility Clinic." *Nursing Inquiry*, vol. 14, no. 2, 2007, pp. 132-39.

Allen, Jordan, and Julia Moore. "Troubling the Functional/Dysfunctional Family Binary Through the Articulation of Functional Family Estrangement." *Western Journal of Communication*, vol. 81, no. 3, 2017, pp. 281-99.

Amin, Nyna. "'She Doesn't Look Like She is Both Mother and Father': Disrupting the Child/Parent Binary." *Agenda: Empowering Women for Gender Equality*, vol. 79, 2009, pp. 24-29.

Bauer, Greta R., et al. "'I Don't Think this is Theoretical; This Is Our Lives': How Erasure Impacts Health Care for Transgender People." *Journal of the Association of Nurses in AIDS Care*, vol. 20, no. 5, 2009, pp. 348-61.

Colapinto, John. *As Nature Made Him: The Boy Who Was Raised as a Girl.* HarperCollins Publishers, 2000.

Cruz, David. "Heterosexual Reproductive Imperatives." *Emory Law Journal*, vol. 56, no. 4, 2007, pp. 1157-72.

Dentice, Dianne, and Michelle Dietert. "Liminal Spaces and Transgender Experience." *Theory in Action*, vol. 8, no. 2, 2015, pp. 69-96.

Douglas, Mary. *Purity and Danger.* Penguin, 1966.

Doussa, Henry von, Jennifer Power, and Damien Riggs. "Imagining Parenthood: The Possibilities and Experiences of Parenthood among Transgender People." *Culture, Health & Sexuality*, vol. 17, no. 9, 2015, pp. 1119-31.

Dowling, Sally, and David Pontin. "Using Liminality to Understand Mothers' Experiences of Long-Term Breastfeeding: 'Betwixt and Between,' and 'Matter out of Place.'" *Health*, vol. 21, no. 1, 1997, pp. 57-75.

Edelman, Lee. *No Future: Queer Theory and the Death Drive.* Duke University Press, 2004.

Fausto-Sterling, Anne. "Gender/Sex, Sexual Orientation and Identity Are in the Body: How Did They Get There?" *The Journal of Sex Research,* vol. 56, no. 4-5, 2019, pp. 1-27.

Fausto-Sterling, Anne. "The Five Sexes, Revisited." *The Sciences,* vol. 40, no. 4, 2000, pp. 18-23.

Feinberg, Leslie. *Transgender Warriors: Making History from Joan of Arc to Dennis Rodman.* Beacon Press, 1996.

Franke, Katherine M. "Theorizing Yes: An Essay on Feminism, Law and Desire." *Columbia Law Review,* vol. 101, 2001, pp. 181-208.

Intersex Society of North America. *Intersex Society of North America.* ISNA, 2008, isna.org/. Accessed 12 Oct. 2021.

Johnson, Austin H. "Transnormativity: A New Concept and its Validation through Documentary Film about Transgender Men. *Sociological Inquiry,* vol. 86, no. 4, 2016, pp. 465-91.

Hughes, Laine. "Wronging the Right-Body Narrative: On the Universality of Gender Uncertainty." *Current Critical Debates in the Field of Transsexual Studies,* edited by Oren Gozlan, Routledge, 2018, pp. 181-93.

Karaian, Lara. "Pregnant Men: Repronormativity, Critical Trans Theory and the Re(conceive)ing of Sex and Pregnancy in Law." *Social and Legal Studies,* vol. 22, no. 2, 2013, pp. 211-30.

Kim, Kyung M., and Se Kwang Hwang. "Being a 'Good' Mother: Immigrant Mothers of Disabled Children." *International Social Work,* vol. 62, no. 4, 2019, pp. 1198-1212.

Kitzinger, Celia, and Jo Willmott. "'The Thief of Womanhood': Women's Experiences of Polycystic Ovarian Syndrome." *Social Science and Medicine,* vol. 54, 2002, pp. 349-61.

Lowik, A.J. "Betwixt, Between, Besides: Reflections on Moving Beyond the Binary in Reproductive Health Care." *Creative Nursing,* vol. 26, no. 2, 2020, pp. 105-08.

Lowik, A.J. "Reproducing Eugenics, Reproducing while Trans: The State Sterilization of Trans People." *Journal of GLBT Family Studies,* vol. 14, no. 5, 2018, pp. 425-45.

Lowik, A.J. "The Ties That Bind are Broken: Trans* Breastfeeding

Practices, Ungendering Body parts and Unsexing Parenting Roles." *Essential Breakthroughs: Conversations about Men, Mothers and Mothering*, edited by Fiona Joy Green and Gary Lee Pelletier, Demeter Press, 2015, pp. 205-21.

Lowik, A.J., Peter Hoong, and Rod Knight. "Where's the Science? A Critical Interrogation of How Sex and Gender are Used to Inform Low-Risk Alcohol Use Guidelines." *Journal of Addiction Medicine*, vol. 14, no. 5, 2020, pp. 357-59.

Marshall, Joyce L., Mary Godfrey, and Mary J. Renfrew. "Being a 'Good Mother': Managing Breastfeeding and Merging Identities." *Social Science & Medicine*, vol. 65, no. 10, 2007, pp. 2147-59.

Murray, Samantha. "Within or Beyond the Binary/Boundary? Intersex Infants and Parental Decisions." *Australian Feminist Studies*, vol. 24, no. 60, 2009, pp. 265-74.

More, Sam Dylan. "The Pregnant Man—An Oxymoron?" *Journal of Gender Studies*, vol. 7, no. 3, 1998, pp. 319-28.

Narcisco, Isabel, et al. "Mapping the 'Good Mother'—Meanings and Experiences in Economically and Socially Disadvantaged Contexts." *Children and Youth Services Review*, vol. 93, 2018, pp. 418-27.

Nentwich, Julia C. "New Fathers and Mothers as Gender Trouble-makers? Exploring Discursive Constructions of Heterosexual Parenthood and their Subversive Potential." *Feminism and Psychology*, vol.18, no. 2, 2008, pp. 207-30.

O'Brien, Jodi. "Heterosexism and Homophobia." *International Encyclopedia of the Social and Behavioral Sciences*, edited by Neil J. Smelser and Paul B. Baltes, Elsevier, 2001, pp. 6672-76.

Poteat, Tonia, Danielle German, and Colin Flynn. "The Conflation of Gender and Sex: Gaps and Opportunities in HIV Data among Transgender Men and MSM." *Global Public Health*, vol. 11, no. 7-8, 2016, pp. 835-48.

Reiheld, Alison. "'The Event That Was Nothing': Miscarriage as a Liminal Event." *Journal of Social Philosophy*, vol. 46, no. 1, 2015, pp. 9-26.

Rich, Adrienne. *Compulsory Heterosexuality and Lesbian Existence*. Onlywomen Press, 1981.

Robertson, Nyk. "The Power and Subjection of Liminality and

Borderlands of Non-Binary Folx." *Gender Forum*, vol. 69, 2018, pp. 45-59.

Snow, R.C. "Sex, Gender and Vulnerability." *Global Public Health: Gender Inequity in Health: Why It Exists and How We Can Change It*, vol. 3, Suppl 1, 2008, pp. 58-74.

T'Sjoen, Guy, Eva Van Caenegem, and Katrien Wierckx. "Transgenderism and Reproduction." *Current Opinion in Endocrinology, Diabetes and Obesity*, vol. 20, no. 6, 2013, pp. 575-79.

Thomasson, Holly. "Gender Differences in Alcohol Metabolism: Physiological Responses to Ethanol." *Recent Developments in Alcoholism, Volume 12: Women and Alcoholism*, edited by Marc Galanter et al., Springer, 2002, pp. 163-79.

Tsui, Elaine Y., and Joy O. Cheng. "When Failed Motherhood Threatens Womanhood: Using Donor-Assisted Conception (DAC) as the Last Resort." *Asian Women*, vol. 34, no. 2, 2018, pp. 33-60.

Turner, Victor W. *The Ritual Process: Structure and Anti-Structure*. Aldine Publishing Co, 1969.

Turner, Victor W. *The Forest of Symbols: Aspects of Ndembu Ritual*. Cornell University Press, 1970.

Valdes, Francisco. "Queers, Sissies, Dykes and Tomboys: Deconstructing the Conflation of 'Sex,' 'Gender,' and 'Sexual Orientation' in Euro-American Law and Society." *California Law Review*, vol. 83, no. 1, 1995, pp. 1-377.

Watson, Gill. "Parental Liminality: A Way of Understanding the Early Experiences of Parents who have a very Preterm Infant." *Journal of Clinical Nursing*, vol. 20, no. 9-10, 2011, pp. 1462-71.

Weissman, Anna L. "Repronormativity and the Reproduction of the Nation-State: The State and Sexuality Collide." *Journal of GLBT Family Studies*, vol. 13, no. 3, 2017, pp. 277-306.

Wierzbicka, Anna. "The English Expressions *Good Boy* and *Good Girl* and Cultural Models of Child Rearing." *Culture & Psychology*, vol. 10, no. 3, 2004, pp. 251-78.

Wilson, Mandy. "'I Am the Prince of Pain, for I Am a Princess in the Brain': Liminal Transgender Identities, Narratives, and the Elimination of Ambiguities." *Sexualities*, vol. 5, no. 4, 2002, pp. 424-48.

Chapter 1

Reflections on a Feminist Childhood from a Non-Binary Adult

Milo Chesnut

My mother was a good feminist. A child of the 1950s and a teen in the 1960s, she experienced a cultural upheaval perhaps unlike any other American generation of the twentieth century. Although she was raised as a proper Protestant, she became a hippie, a radical socialist, and then a feminist. In the early 1970s, she returned home wearing a short tunic embroidered with flowers and a pair of black leather military boots. My grandmother slammed the door in her face. In the early 1980s, she was wearing stiff shoulder pads and building a career as a graphic designer in New York City. She met a photographer, who would eventually become my father, at a concert. She described their early relationship as fun and casual. He seemed to admire her bold humour and confidence, and took handsome portraits of her, with short brown hair, a vest and a silk green bowtie. In the late 1980s, when digital advances in photography and graphic design were shrinking their career options, they decided to move upstate to a majority white, working-class neighbourhood in rural New York, get married, and have their first child. That was me.

In the 1970s and 1980s, second-wave feminist activists and academics challenged the traditional approach to raising children and, in particular, girls. I must note that although people who may today identify as transgender women did participate in branches of second-wave feminism (Heaney), the vast majority of organizing was focused on the experiences of cisgender girls and women. Through conscious-ness-raising groups, some feminists drew on the collective experience of girlhood to develop a critique of girls' "socialization" (Statham).

However, socialization was originally a concept developed by social learning theorists, who believed that gendered behaviours were learned, just like any other behaviour (Mischel). For example, children might observe their father giving their mother a compliment for trying on a dress. Both boys and girls might then learn that wearing dresses leads to positive attention. However, when boys and girls attempt the behaviours they observe, they often receive "differential reinforcement" from parents, peers, teachers, and others. Children may learn to anticipate which behaviours are "appropriate" for their genders through various experiences of reward and punishment (Kessler and McKenna). The labels of "boy" and "girl" come to stand for the collection of rewarded behaviours, and children begin to value these labels as a part of their self-concept. For social learning theorists, gender identity was not innate, but a result of a process of social conditioning that began with assigned sex at birth (Kohlberg).

Before feminists challenged this traditional process of socialization, social learning theorists recommended that parents socialize their children appropriately (Kessler and McKenna). Implicit in this advice was the moral superiority of a patriarchal two-parent heterosexual family and the active reinforcement of a gender binary based on assigned sex. Contemporary advocates of family values continue to promote elements of the idealized traditional family form (Mack-Canty and Wright). However, the notion that traditional gendered behaviour and identity are learned leaves room for the possibility of unlearning. In this way, socialization became a central element of second-wave feminist organizing and theory (Jackson and Scott).

Although some feminists viewed traditional socialization as a root of women's oppression, they also saw potential in the notion that gender is socially conditioned (Martin). At first, they aimed to reform the socialization of girls, demanding that girls have equal access to items and activities that were previously reserved for boys, such as science, sports, and short hair (Martin). They also advocated for limiting the tools of traditional feminine socialization, such as makeup, house-work, fairy tales, and dresses (Martin). Second-wave feminists called this approach "gender-neutral" or "nonsexist" childrearing (Martin;

Statham). Instead of reinforcing binary gender roles, socialization could be a tool for dismantling patriarchal structures and building a more equitable society.

Liberal feminists, who promoted equality between cisgender men and women, slightly shifted the emphasis of gender-neutral child-rearing (Martin). They sought to remedy the differential socialization of boys as well as girls (Martin). The goal was to neutralize, rather than exaggerate, socialized differences between boys and girls. Differential reinforcement of their behaviour was discouraged, and parents were challenged to positively reinforce gender nonconformity. Since children's observations of their parents played a central role in social learning theory, parents were also encouraged to model egalitarian relationships (Martin; Risman).

Feminists popularized a gender-neutral parenting model through various publications (Martin). The cover of the premiere issue of *Ms.* magazine in 1972 displayed the title "On Raising Kids Without Sex Roles" (Martin). With the support of founder and author Letty Cottin Pogrebin, *Ms.* continued to offer pieces on nonsexist childrearing, reviewed children's toys, and published a recurring column called "Stories for Free Children." This first issue also included a gender-neutral children's story by Lois Gould called "X: A Fabulous Child's Story," which would inspire further iterations of gender-neutral parenting in the early 2010s (Green and Friedman). Between the late 1970s and early 1980s, feminists continued to disseminate their parenting approaches by publishing books and articles that brought gender-neutral parenting to the American mainstream.

I was born in this context. On February 19, 1988, the doctor took a look at me and said I was a girl. My parents agreed. However, as a good feminist, my mom intended to maximize the possibilities available for me, at least within our family's means. My dad was never one to question this plan, unless money was an issue. They aimed to expose me to a range of gendered experiences, offering me tools and trucks as well as stuffed animals and dolls. They preferred to dress me in overalls, just like baby X (Gould). They accumulated a costume trunk full of a range of hand-me-downs and thrift store finds, including funky jewelry and bowties. They encouraged interests in science and art and made sure to describe me with a breadth of adjectives, such as smart, athletic, strong, pretty, creative, and unique. They wanted me to believe that I could be anything I wanted when I grew up.

As grateful as I am for the early freedom to discover my interests and desires without gendered pressure, my family did not exist in isolation. Karen Martin asserts that liberal feminists curbed the potential of gender-neutral parenting in several ways, which she calls "shortcomings." The first was by marketing the approach as a means of individual improvement rather than as a strategy for collective social change (Martin). Originally, feminists believed that gender-neutral socialization held the potential to cultivate an equitable society by diminishing the differences between men and women. However, in order to appeal to the mainstream, liberal feminists marketed publications that framed gender-neutral parenting as a method of raising happy and successful individuals (Martin). An example of this approach was *Free to Be You and Me,* published in 1974, which became one of the most influential liberal feminist parenting publications as a *New York Times* bestselling children's book, record, and television special. These publications obscured the vision of a liberated society that gender-neutral childrearing had once illuminated because they were ultimately focused on the individualist goal of "raising free children" (Martin 460).

However, collectivist social movements have long asserted that none of us are free until everybody is free. Like many children of feminist upbringing, I was first confronted by this paradox at school (see Green and Friedman; Kane, *The Gender Trap*; Mack-Canty and Wright; Statham). I quickly realized that other kids and parents didn't share my mom's egalitarian or feminist values. Every single day on the school bus, I was asked if I was a boy or a girl. I could tell by the laughter and repeated questioning that they were trying to be mean. They wanted to remind me that I was failing at something very basic, something that they all did with apparent ease. When I told my mom what they were doing, she turned red and said, "Well they're all idiots; of course, you're a girl!" I didn't understand why at the time, but her response made me feel worse.

There were many other moments throughout my childhood where I unintentionally hit the limit of what was acceptable for a girl in that particular time and place: when I raised my hand too much in class, when I beat the boys at sports, when I cut my hair short, when I tried out for the lead role of Nathan Detroit in *Guys and Dolls,* or when I played basketball shirtless with my best friend right at the onset of puberty. My mom continued to support me, defending my right to be a different kind of girl. But even she had her limit to the possibilities of what a girl could be. At seventeen years old, I came out as gay, and she burst into tears. I asked her why she was crying, and she said because now she knew she wouldn't have grandchildren. I was shocked and confused. Why would she assume that I would want to birth children even if I were straight? Why did she think that being gay meant I wouldn't want children?

In retrospect, my mother's response was not that surprising. Martin explains that the second shortcoming of second-wave gender-neutral childrearing was that liberal feminists did not fully unpack the relationship between sexuality and gender. As a result, homophobic and heterosexist ideas remained in the literature that advised parents about gender-neutrality in the 1970s and 1980s. In part, this was a marketing decision. Feminist writers such as Cottin Pogrebin and Selma Betty Greenberg were aware that the common assumption that gender nonconforming behaviour in children would lead to homosexuality was a major barrier to the widespread uptake of gender-neutral parenting. This was evident in Cottin Pogrebin's 1980 article in *Ms.* Magazine titled "The Secret Fear That Keeps Us from Raising Free Children." To assuage parents' fears that gender-neutral parenting would cultivate homosexual tendencies, Cottin Pogrebin attempted to dispel harmful misunderstandings about the connection between gender and sexuality. However, the article also capitalized on mainstream homophobia by suggesting that gender-neutral parenting might even prevent homosexuality. A similar argument emerges in Greenberg's book, *Right from the Start,* published in 1978. Greenberg insists that there is nothing wrong with homosexuality and that homophobia from parents and schools will harm children. However, Greenberg goes on to state that fathers "whose relations are positive, warm, and nurturing do not tend to have sons who grow up to be adult homosexuals" (qtd. in Martin 46). Again, parental fears of homosexuality were exploited to promote gender-neutral parenting. Both of these authors also use scientific research from the fields of medicine and psychology to bolster their claims (Cottin Pogrebin; Greenberg). These examples show that unfortunately, while promoting gender-neutral childrearing, liberal feminists continued to frame homosexuality as problematic.

Perhaps this contextualizes how my mother could support my gender nonconforming behaviour without imagining the possibility of a child who was something other than straight. She was always offended when anyone would suggest or assume that I might not be straight, suggesting that I was just a child and how could they tell? Although I appreciated the attempt to dispel potentially stereotypical assumptions about my childhood sexuality based on my gender expression, I also sensed that both my parents imagined and preferred a straight future for me. I picked up on their comments, jokes, discomforts, and inconsistencies. Some were explicit, and some were subtle, but without direct support for a future I could already tell was discouraged by the culture around me, I got the message that being gay was not okay. By the time I came out at seventeen, I had already struggled for years with fear of how my parents would respond. The stress of that time still affects me as an adult, and many people have experienced far worse. With all of the freedom to discover my interests and desires as a child, what a difference it would have made if that freedom had extended to my sexuality.

In addition to individualism and heterosexism, I argue that a third shortcoming of the second-wave feminist conceptualization of gender-neutral parenting was the unquestioned binary sex system. By advocating for gender-neutrality, second-wave feminists were challenging the advice of many scientists, psychologists, and medical professionals who insisted that traditional socialization was the only way to raise well-adjusted children (Martin). However, they stopped short of questioning the practice of assigning sex at birth and continued to define males and females based on the same criteria used by the medical establishment. This shortcoming was a missed opportunity to connect feminist analysis to the struggles of intersex and transgender communities, who were also greatly affected by traditional approaches to socialization.

Unfortunately, beginning in the 1960s, social scientists were applying theories of gender socialization to the bodies of infants (Fausto-Sterling). Babies born with genitalia that was not easily categorized as male or female were given risky surgeries to ensure that their bodies conformed to an idealized binary aesthetic. Parents were then advised to raise their children as the gender that was assumed to correspond to their surgically altered genitals. The doctors and scientists theorized that babies socialized as a certain gender would grow to identify with that gender, but that was not always the case (Diamond and Sigmundson). These so-called normalizing surgeries are still performed on intersex babies today, often without the informed consent of parents and never with the consent of the children (Davis; Lohman and Lohman). The potential consequences of these surgeries include loss of sensitivity, sterilization, and various forms of psychological distress (Lohman and Lohman; Pagonis). Intersex advocates have made gains towards the abolition of these normalizing surgeries on infants, such as statements of support from the United Nations and World Health Organization, but the surgeries continue to be performed around the world (Lohman and Lohman). Second-wave feminists who advocated for gender-neutral parenting challenged the imperative for girls to be socialized differently than boys, but they did not question the division of all of humanity into either male or female sex categories. This oversight contributed to an erasure of intersex experience and struggle as well as a failure to question the heart of the binary sex system—assigning sex at birth.

The possibility of transgender experience was also ignored in second-wave feminist gender-neutral parenting conceptualizations. For example, the bestselling children's book *Free to Be You and Me* was typical of liberal feminist ideals in that it was filled with stories and songs assuring boys and girls that they were entitled to a full range of emotional and career options. Although the introduction boasts that "anyone could be anything," there were some clear limitations. One poem called "Parents are People" reads as follows:

Some mommies are ranchers
Or poetry makers
Or doctors or teachers
Or cleaners or bakers.
Some mommies drive taxis
Or sing on TV.
Yes, mommies can be
Almost anything they want to be.

They can't be grandfathers
Or daddies... (my emphasis; Thomas 48)

The poem continues to place the reverse restraint on the gendered futures of "daddies." Although the collection overall questions traditional binary gender roles, assigned sex remains a stable and unchallenged category, precluding the possibility of trans, non-binary, or intersex experience.

The notion that assigned sex alone is the defining characteristic of boys and girls is echoed in the work of Sandra Bem, an influential feminist psychologist who promoted the concept of "psychological androgyny"—the socialization of both masculine and feminine traits and interests in children in order to undermine "gender role polar-ization" and increase positive outcomes (Dean and Tate 643). In the 1980s, Bem provided advice to parents on raising children outside of the constraints of traditional gender roles, which included teaching children that reproductive anatomy and secondary sex characteristics were the only differences between boys and girls (Liben and Bigler). Bem implemented these strategies as a parent and recounted that when her son Jeremy's classmate accused him of being a girl because he was wearing barrettes at nursery school, he replied, "Wearing barrettes doesn't matter. I have a penis and testicles," and then " he pulled down his pants to make his point more convincingly" ("Gender Schema Theory" 612). The peer, who apparently had received different lessons about gender, was not convinced, and responded, "Everybody has a penis; only girls wear barrettes" ("Gender Schema Theory" 612). Besides exemplifying that children sometimes conceptualize gender differently than adults (Kessler and McKenna), this anecdote again highlights a key limitation of the second-wave promotion of gender neutrality. By defining sex solely on the basis of anatomy, Bem opens up many possibilities for gendered expression. However, this approach also reduces gender identity down to the appearance of genitals, excluding the possibility of bodily self-definition and ignoring the existence of intersex bodies.

My parents took a similar approach. I was raised in an environment that encouraged experimentation and play with gender. Although my behaviour might have been perceived as gender nonconforming to others, my parents treated me as a unique and creative individual. When I was three years old, my mom asked me what I wanted to be for Halloween, and I said, "a little old man." In one of my favourite childhood pictures, I am dressed as a small gentleman, complete with moustache and cane. I don't remember any negative reactions to my costume choice, only the feeling of cohesion as I gripped my little cane and put on my bowler hat. Some of my favourite toys at that time were a wooden tool set and a plastic baby doll. I named my doll "Jacob," despite anatomy that a doctor would likely assign female, and my mom didn't mention that there was anything odd about that until years later when I came out as non-binary.

In retrospect, I am deeply grateful that my parents let me lead without fear that gender experimentation would inevitably cause some undesirable future. After all, why can't little girls be attracted to tools and bowler hats? However, their openness was based on similar beliefs as the poem above—that no matter how much I transgressed traditional gender expectations, I would always be a girl. This vision of girlness is expansive but bound by assigned sex. As open-minded and progressive as my parents were, I don't think they ever considered that I would grow up to identify as anything other than a woman.

Many studies have shown that kids who are assigned female at birth are often allowed more gender transgression than those who are assigned male, at least in Western cultures (Kane, "No Way"; Meadow; Travers). Perhaps this is because masculinity is culturally valued more than femininity or evidence of second-wave feminism's effect on the way girls are socialized (Meadow). However, parental endorsement of their daughters' gender play may have an expiration date. For me, that moment was puberty. Although I was still encouraged to display a range of "psychologically androgynous" traits, such as assertiveness and compassion, and to pursue whichever career I was drawn to, my persistent attraction to clothes typically reserved for men eventually became a source of tension.

I remember the rising joy in my body when I found the tuxedo in the back of the Salvation Army. After a lifetime of thrifting, I knew that some days were good, and some were bad, but you just had to keep looking. It struck me as I stared into the mirror in the dressing room that this tuxedo was perhaps the best find of my life. I searched my reflection for the usual problems: oversized shoulders, stretching around the chest and hips, legs so long I could trip, but it fit like a second skin. It was as if it were made for me, and I could afford the fifteen dollars with my new job. I knew exactly where I was going to wear it.

Although my mom encouraged her three-year-old daughter to "play dress-up" in suits and ties, she balked at her fifteen-year-old teenager asking to wear a tuxedo to the school dance. My stomach dropped as she explained that I would distract from everyone else's experience and draw too much attention to myself. I pushed back, but she insisted that I would make everyone else uncomfortable. Eventually, I gave in to the growing feeling of shame and agreed to wear a simple black velvet dress instead.

Looking back, I don't fully know what my mom was thinking or feeling when she refused to let me wear my tuxedo. However, studies have shown that parents of gender nonconforming and transgender children often engage in a process termed "gender hedging" (Rahilly). Gender hedging is when parents weigh the potential for bullying and harassment against the possible harm caused by stifling their children's gender expression, working to find compromises that they hope will better ensure their safety (Rahilly; Kane, *The Gender Trap*). Perhaps in a different context, where the culture of bullying hadn't already inflicted lasting wounds, my mom would have felt differently about my tuxedo. She may also simply have been embarrassed, worried about what other parents would say. Or perhaps, deep down, she believed she could still redirect me onto a more feminine path. Whatever the underlying reason, I was left with an impression that gender transgression was no longer acceptable.

By the mid-1980s, socialization fell out of favour as a framework for understanding gender development for several reasons (Martin). First, the mainstream liberal feminist version of gender-neutral socialization failed to radically upend gender structures (Martin). Second, childhood sociologists critiqued socialization for overlooking children's agency in their own gendering (Thorne). Socialization theory often conceptualized children as blank slates with no will of their own (Martin). I also argue that the rise in transgender activism in the early 1990s centred the subjective experiences of individuals whose transgender selves persisted in the face of aggressive traditional socialization attempts. Seminal transgender scholars—such as Sandy Stone, Susan Stryker, Riki Wilchins, Leslie Feinberg, and Kate Bornstein—rightly critiqued feminist theories that naturalized binary sex categories, leading to further divisions in feminist movements that persist today.

A notable example of a second-wave gender-neutral parenting

advocate with a change of heart was Sandra Bem. As discussed earlier, Bem originally advocated for minimizing the presence of gendered polarization in social life by teaching children that "a boy is someone with a penis and testicles, and a girl is someone with a clitoris, vagina, and a uterus; and whether you're a girl or boy, a man or a woman, doesn't need to matter" ("Dismantling Gender Polarization" 330). However, in 1995, Bem was influenced by transgender, queer, and intersex scholarship to reform her position: "Let 1,000 categories of sex/gender/desire bloom. Through that proliferation, we can undo the privileged status of the two-and-only-two categories that are currently treated as normal and natural" ("Dismantling Gender Polarization" 330).

Unfortunately, it took two decades for shifts in gender theory and the efforts of the growing trans rights movement to influence my family. It wasn't until my early twenties, after majoring in gender and queer studies in college, that I found language to describe my gender that fit as well as my first tuxedo. I have accepted that this language may change over time and that my gender identity—and to a certain extent, my body—can be as expansive as my gender expression. Perhaps the early openness of my parents' approach to gender enabled me to more freely adopt and express new ideas.

In 2011, I read an article about Storm—a child whose parents were inspired by *X: A Fabulous Child's Story*—to raise their children with they/them/their pronouns from birth (James). I realized that my childhood could never have been truly gender-neutral because my parents and the world around me still attributed a gender identity to my assigned sex. Furthermore, Storm's parents were not aiming for a neutral environment but a balanced exposure to a range of gendered experiences. By not assuming a gender identity for Storm, they were also making space for their child to self-determine their own identity. With the explicit support to explore and experiment with pronouns and identities, Storm may never have to feel the fear of coming out as trans or non-binary to their parents. Parents who hold no expectations about gender must also be open to a range of possible sexualities. Something clicked, and I could envision myself as a parent for the first time.

Now I'm thirty-two years old. I am working on a PhD, researching the "theyby" parenting movement that has grown since Storm's story was published. Theyby parents—also known as "gender open," "gender creative," "gender independent," and many other evolving terms—raise their babies with they/them/their pronouns from birth in order to resist the barrage of assumptions associated with assigned sex. Many theyby parents also challenge the practice of assigning sex at birth, advocating to remove assigned sex from birth certificates or leave the field blank. I am hopeful that the framing of nonconsensual gendering as harmful and the insistence that children have the right to determine their own sex and gender could benefit all children, especially transgender and intersex children.

Although I do not currently have children, I have taken steps with my partner to begin the process. As I continue to learn about gender-open parenting, I am constantly reflecting on my own childhood and imagining my possible future as a parent. I experienced both the benefits and the shortcomings of the second-wave feminist manifest-ation of gender-neutral parenting. Even though I am deeply grateful for my parents' expansive definition of "girl" and their persistent encour-agement, the impact of the limitations of individualism, heterosexism, and cisnormativity (if not transphobia) were deep and long lasting. I believe that if parents are invested in raising free children, then those children must be free to explore and express themselves to the fullest extent.

I want to learn from my experiences and ensure that my children know that I will never place limitations on them based on assumptions about what their bodies mean. In addition to the obvious benefit to children like me, maybe my parents could have also benefitted from their own reflexive exercise about the practice of gendering children based on assigned sex or assigning sex at all. For example, if my parents hadn't assumed that I would grow up to be straight and have children, maybe they wouldn't have felt so much pain when I came out as gay. If they hadn't expected me to grow up to be a woman, maybe they wouldn't have felt confused or disappointed when I asked them to use they/them/their pronouns. If they had seen me as more autonomous, maybe it wouldn't have hurt when I changed the name they gave me, a name they loved, for one of my own choosing.

However, I am always wary of perpetuating a mother-blame narrative. Feminists have argued that the so-called good mother is an idealized, quixotic construction of an innate nurturer who selflessly loves her children unconditionally, without any concern for her own wellbeing or ambitions. When mothers struggle to obtain this unachievable ideal, the individual mother is blamed for her failure in a system that is rigged against her. Rather than fostering solidarity and collective action around oppressive institutions, discourses of "good" and "bad" mothering invite individual mothers to turn against one another, widening social and economic divisions (Jensen).

Similarly, I do not intend to propose that all of society's problems, or even just my problems, could be solved if parents simply made different choices. This argument would fall under the same individualist thinking that stunted the second-wave liberal feminist concept-ualization of gender-neutral parenting. "Choice" is a critical organizing principle in neoliberal society, which obscures the material conditions in which choices are made (Jensen). Parenting has become neo-liberalized in the sense that parental choices and personal conduct have been positioned as the central factors in determining children's outcomes—even more important than material conditions (such as income, healthcare, and housing) and larger social institutions (such as formal education) (Jensen). Thus, individual families are held morally accountable for the conditions of poverty, precarity, and disen-franchisement within which they make their choices (Jensen).

With this in mind, parenting sounds really difficult. I certainly recognize that there were structural limitations placed on my family, particularly my mother. Although my parents were afforded the privileges of whiteness in the United States and my mother had attended college, they struggled financially. My mother worked full-time throughout my childhood while taking on the second-shift of caregiver. She creatively drew on the resources around her, making toys out of cardboard cereal boxes and aluminum foil and acquiring hand-me-downs from neighbours and scholarships for me to attend camp. When it was time for college, she argued with my dad to take on enormous debt so that I could attend my top-choice school. I recognize the emphasis on my mom in my memories and writing as well as the increased responsibility I grant her as my primary caregiver. These structural challenges my mom faced, even as a parent with relative privilege, shaped the choices that were available to her. Many other parents are constrained by far more, and parenting alone will not dismantle these structural barriers.

The feminists who originally envisioned gender-neutral parenting as a path to collective liberation believed that shifts in socialization needed to be accompanied by efforts to promote equity in the culture at large. Emily Kane, author of *The Gender Trap: Parents and the Pitfalls of Raising Boys and Girls*, explains that "parents cannot do it alone" and that "a sociological perspective reveals a need for a collective effort of multiple social actors and social institutions" (201). I know from personal experience that the choices parents make to cultivate environments where children feel encouraged to explore their gender and sexuality are deeply meaningful. However, these efforts must be accompanied by collective actions that challenge the structural barriers to gender self-determination for all parents.

Works Cited

Bem, Sandra Lipsitz. "Gender Schema Theory and Its Implications for Child Development: Raising Gender-Aschematic Children in a Gender-Schematic Society." *Signs*, vol. 8, no. 4, 1983, pp. 598-616.

Bem, Sandra Lipsitz. "Dismantling Gender Polarization and Compulsory Heterosexuality: Should We Turn the Volume Down or Up?" *Journal of Sex Research*, vol. 32, no. 4, 1995, pp. 329-34.

Bornstein, Kate. *Gender Outlaw: On Men, Women, and the Rest of Us.* Routledge, 1994.

Davis, Georgiann. *Contesting Intersex: The Dubious Diagnosis.* NYU Press, 2015. *JSTOR*, www.jstor.org/stable/j.ctt15zc7ht. Accessed 16 Feb. 2020.

Dean, M. Lee, and Charlotte Chucky Tate. "Extending the Legacy of Sandra Bem: Psychological Androgyny as a Touchstone Conceptual Advance for the Study of Gender in Psychological Science." *Sex Roles*, vol. 76, no. 11-12, 2016, pp. 1-12.

Fausto-Sterling, Anne. *Sexing the Body: Gender Politics and the Construction of Sexuality.* Basic Books, 2000.

Feinberg, Leslie. "Transgender Liberation: A Movement Whose Time Has Come." *The Transgender Studies Reader*, edited by Susan Stryker and Stephen Whittle, Routledge, 2006, pp. 205-220.

Gould, Lois. "X: A Fabulous Child's Story." *Women: Images and Realities: A Multicultural Anthology*, edited by Amy Kesselman, Lily

McNair, and Nancy Schneidewind. Mayfield Publishing Company, 1997, pp. 108-13.

Green, Fiona Joy, and May Friedman. *Chasing Rainbows: Exploring Gender Fluid Parenting Practices.* Demeter Press, 2013.

Greenberg, Selma Betty. *Right from the Start: A Guide to Nonsexist Child Rearing.* Houghton Mifflin Harcourt (HMH), 1978.

Heaney, Emma. "Women-Identified Women: Trans Women in 1970s Lesbian Feminist Organizing." *TSQ: Transgender Studies Quarterly,* vol. 3, no. 1-2, 2016, p. 137.

Jackson, Stevi, and Sue Scott. *Feminism and Sexuality: A Reader.* Edinburgh University Press, 1996.

James, Susan D. "Baby Storm Raised Genderless Is Bad Experiment, Says Experts." *ABC News,* 2011, abcnews.go.com/Health/baby-storm-raised-genderless-gender-dangerous-experiment-child/story?id=13693760. Accessed 16 Oct. 2021.

Jensen, Tracey. *Parenting the Crisis: The Cultural Politics of Parent-Blame.* Policy Press, 2018.

Kane, Emily. "'No Way My Boys Are Going to Be Like That!': Parents' Responses to Children's Gender Nonconformity." *Gender & Society,* vol. 20, no. 2, 2006, pp. 149-76.

Kane, Emily. *The Gender Trap: Parents and the Pitfalls of Raising Boys and Girls.* New York University Press, 2012.

Kessler, Susan J., and Wendy McKenna. *Gender: An Ethnomethodological Approach.* Wiley, 1978.

Kohlberg, Lawrence. "A Cognitive-Developmental Analysis of Children's Sex Role Concepts and Attitudes." *The Development of Sex Differences,* edited by Eleanor Macoby, Stanford University Press, 1966, pp. 82-173.

Liben, Lynn S., and Rebecca S. Bigler. "Understanding and Undermining the Development of Gender Dichotomies: The Legacy of Sandra Lipsitz Bem." *Sex Roles,* vol. 76, no. 9-10, 2017, pp. 544-55.

Lohman, Eric, and Stephani Lohman. *Raising Rosie: Our Story of Parenting an Intersex Child.* Jessica Kingsley Publishers, 2018.

Mack-Canty, Colleen, and Sue Wright. "Family Values as Practiced by Feminist Parents: Bridging Third-Wave Feminism and Family Pluralism." *Journal of Family Issues,* vol. 25, no. 7, 2004, pp. 851-80.

Martin, Karin A. "William Wants a Doll. Can He Have One? Feminists, Child Care Advisors, and Gender-Neutral Child Rearing. (Author Abstract)." *Gender & Society*, vol. 19, no. 4, 2005, p. 456.

Meadow, Tey. *Trans Kids: Being Gendered in the Twenty-First Century.* University of California Press, 2018.

Mischel, Walter. "A Social-Learning View of Sex Differences in Behavior." *The Development of Sex Differences*, vol. 56, 1966, p. 81.

Pagonis, Pidgeon, director. *Hi, I'm Intersex—Part 3 (Clitorectomy).* YouTube, 21 Nov. 2016, www.youtube.com/watch?v=dUmmPftumn U. Accessed Oct. 16 2021.

Pogrebin, Letty Cottin. *Growing up Free: Raising Your Child in the 80's.* McGraw-Hill, 1980.

Rahilly, Elizabeth. "The Gender Binary Meets the Gender-Variant Child: Parents' Negotiations with Childhood Gender Variance." *Gender and Society*, vol. 29, no. 3, 2015, pp. 338-61.

Risman, Barbara, and Kristen Myers. "As the Twig Is Bent: Children Reared in Feminist Households." *Qualitative Sociology*, vol. 20, no. 2, 1997, pp. 229-52.

Skeggs, Beverley. *Class, Self, Culture.* Routledge, 2003.

Statham, June. *Daughters and Sons: Experiences of Non-Sexist Childraising.* B. Blackwell, 1986.

Stone, Sandy. "The Empire Strikes Back." *Sandy Stone*, 1994, sandystone.com/empire-strikes-back.pdf. Accessed 16 Oct. 2021.

Stryker, Susan. "My Words to Victor Frankenstein Above the Village of Chamounix: Performing Transgender Rage." *GLQ: A Journal of Lesbian & Gay*, vol. 1, no. 3, 1993, pp. 237-54.

Thomas, Marlo. *Free to Be... You and Me.* McGraw-Hill, 1974.

Thorne, Barrie. *Gender Play: Girls and Boys in School.* Open University Press, 1993. Print.

Travers, Ann. *The Trans Generation: How Trans Kids (and Their Parents) Are Creating a Gender Revolution.* New York University Press, 2018.

Wilchins, Riki. *Read My Lips: Sexual Subversion and the End of Gender.* Firebrand Books, 1997.

Chapter 2

Baby Triptych

Eitan Codish

Artist's Statement

This was not the poem series that I set out to write. I intended for it to have much more form— evenly spaced poems of similar structure tracking my child's development at one-month intervals over their first six months of life. What came out was more authentic to the experience of parenting a child with queer values than what I could have hoped for. It starts with the unformed (you), gains cohesiveness in the naming sonnet, and then stretches across the page in chaotic growth in the final section, which was written when my little one, now almost two years old, was just five months.

The poem doesn't need to say that my child has no gender. The intent is to embody parental love and authentic growth of all of the individuals involved in that love. "You" and "I" and "We" are all ungendered pronouns, and this poem exists within the realm of the relationship; pronouns that convey gender are only used when explaining out, and a good poem doesn't need to explain. I didn't want the absence of gender to become a presence in itself; I simply allowed the presence of the child and parent to fill the space such that gender never became a question.

1. Conceiving

(You) invited me into your home before it was built

(You) in the loft above the scratched bed of the pick up

(You) a warm pool by a cold river

(You) a cold room in the basement of a warm house

(You) rough and sweet like berry bushes

(You) fighting back the forest and getting entwined

(You) a distant beach, scalding and magnetic

(You) held me inside while I turned inside out

(You) amphibious toes like ferny tendrils cling to slick rock

(You) the size of a seed, the breadth of silence

2. Naming

The nine-month night you learned your names
while we waited on their prisms,
how they would refract
like the scripts that write them
twirl like your hair, clockwise and counter

The moon full, you emerged a crescent
reflected in the warm pool
in our cool basement,
a hiddenness arched to draw out,
to preserve, take, and bring forth

Q, you will carry these names:
ones that are given to you by us,
ones others call you
and ones that you create for yourself

3. Feeding

I am my love's; my love is mine

all our parts shift

               crack stretch compress
               turn and tilt toward

       your face

                    your eyes of no
                        particular colour

     the line   between
        desire
    need   obligation fades

                 what you consume we continue to carry
                    our   bodies   your   weight
                 the eyes and voices we bring in

       to focus

    mirror   your newest gurgle
                tight grasp expanding reach and nuance

   calming jostle of constant flight
the knowledge that movement is life

Chapter 3

Motherhood Is Speculative (Non)Fiction

Kamee Abrahamian

THIS IS NOT A DISCLAIMER: I came into existence amid two layers of denial: as the descendant of Armenian genocide survivors displaced from Lebanon and Syria and as a first-generation Canadian born onto lands painfully colonized through the genocide of Indigenous peoples. Motherhood is speculative (non)fiction is a rhizomatic writing experiment that explores the expanded way-of-being-in-the-world of new motherhood as I have experienced it. The piece is first and foremost personal and draws from the landscape of my intersectional experiences and sensibilities as a queer, South West Asian, North African (SWANA[1]), and diasporic mother. I arrive at queerness (and motherhood) in the same way as described by queer, feminist scholar of colour Alexis Pauline Gumbs as what "fundamentally transforms our state of being and the possibilities for life ... does not produce the status quo" (115). It is the lens through which I understand my being in the world and how I build relationships and work in/with communities. And identifying as queer, feminist, and non-normative has situated me on the fringes of my own cultural community and, on most days, in the world.

As a work in-progress, my writing here takes shape through an iteration of "rhizovocality"—as put forth by Alecia Youngblood Jackson—in how the reading is sculpted through a constantly interrupted flow resulting from my everyday life as primary caregiver for my first baby. Jackson writes the following:

These multiple entryways for understanding are acentered, nonhierarchical, temporal, productive, and exist in the middle; thus, rhizovocality can be neither fully transcendent nor authentic since it has no original departure or destined arrival. Rhizovocality "is perpetually in construction or collapsing ... a process that is perpetually prolonging itself, breaking off and starting again ... connecting any point to any other point" (Deleuze and Guattari 20-21) (707).

Jackson refers to Deleuze and Guattari's image of the rhizome and invites readers to imagine beyond the dominant linearity of thinking and writing. This is echoed in my writing as I perpetually unravel, and it becomes clear that this process is also a reflection of my psychological and embodied experience of time, gender, and relationality—one that I am only just beginning to untangle and articulate. For this reason, I understand my version of motherhood as speculative (non)fiction, in how it always aspires towards restoring the both-ness (queer and brown, gendered and ungendered, temporal and atemporal, etc.) of my lived experience. And so, in the grander scheme of things, motherhood will be forever iterative and cyclical.

This concept of ceaseless construction-collapse resonates in my experiences as a mother in what I call "constellated fragmentation." I write *in pieces*, during my little one's (Saana) sporadic naptimes and on the rare occasion that my partner or friend is able to care for them. It is nearly impossible to find a moment or headspace to sit with the entirety of this endeavour or to trace the epic thread(s) that tie it all together. I am constantly tethered, in body and self, to my child and to motherhood, much like the moon in its eternal orbit around earth. This is not a disclaimer but the paradigmatic reality of my current existence. For these reasons, I have chosen to write pieces of prose weaved with thoughts that reflect some of my own thinking, interspersed with those of others. My style and practice draw from and build upon an interdisciplinary body of work—the artmaking, writing, as well as the social justice and healing work of queers, radical feminists, and people of colour. The biomythography genre by Audre Lorde is particularly influential, as this piece similarly combines history, biography, and mythmaking. Armen Ohanian's memoirs are also an inspiration. In my own reading and working with her work, I have always imagined her writing as creative nonfiction, one that tells truth through fantasy.

My state of mind while writing much of this, especially the prose, was surely fantastical in more ways than one. I am also a big fan of science-fiction, which may come through in the prose that is weaved throughout this piece. My intention here is to experiment and hone in on my own style and genre.

In "The Birth of a Mother," Alexandra Sacks introduced me to "matrescence"—a predominantly anthropological term coined by Dana Raphael that refers to the identity shift and transitional process of becoming a mother. For me, this transition (although I do not perceive of it as necessarily anthropological) has been both an incredibly challenging and profoundly expansive experience. In the writing below, I attempt to track this transition here. Parsing through my thoughts around how motherhood has also affected my own process of individuation or, rather, of becoming-aware-of-my-becoming. And this process has also overlapped with my study and integration of decolonial philosophy, critical queer theory, and feminism. The intersection of becoming and philosophizing has led me to understand my own matrescence as also being heavily influenced by what Maria Lugones describes as "micro-resistances" and "world-travelling." My world in this context is my own body and my family constellation, or those whom I orbit with. Micro-resistances become the minutiae and the rhizomatic function inside my positionality as a new mother.

I am interested in how the consciousness of a new mother is affected by the coloniality of time and gender—in how the experience of becoming and being-in-the-world of a new mother inherently requires world-travelling—to inhabit multiple worlds/timelines, social constructions, and experiences at once. All of a sudden, a new mother becomes a mother according to capitalism, a mother according to colonialism, a mother according to values, a mother according to mainstream media, and so on—all the while negotiating a complex and demanding relationship with another (who is not quite yet an other). I am interested in queer motherhood. I am interested in microcurrents of power and power differentials as they relate to gender and dominant conceptions and expectations of gender inherited through social transactions between parents and others (family, friends, strangers, etc.). I am interested in how all this happens. I am interested in how there is so much literature out there dedicated to understanding and undoing gender, yet in my experience thus far, there is a serious lack of contemporary writing in the realm of psychology and philosophy of how gender comes to be inside the relations and process of parenting and caregiving of children in general. There is more to say here, but I am running out of time because Saana is about to wake up. I would rather move forward with the doing rather than writing about the doing.

> I sit on a rug my grandfather passed down to me after Saana was born. It is red, yellow, black. Saana is nine months old now. They are naked, teething, miserable. Today has been miserable. Earlier this morning I told my partner, "I'm going to get some herbs from the garden." It had just rained. When I reached the rosemary bush, I stopped, looked at the scissors in my hands, and wondered if they were sharp enough to cut through vein. I thought about crying, hoping it would help, but milk poured out of my eyes and onto the wet grass, disappearing into the earth forever.
>
> This rug is red, yellow, black, old. It is magic. This is a mother-fucking magic carpet. It is here, on this carpet, sitting cross legged with one hand hovering behind Saana ready to catch their fall, when the clearest thought since my first sleepless night arrived in my mind: queer motherhood is speculative (non)fiction.[2]

Speculative fiction is an umbrella term that includes (but is not limited to) narrative genres, such as science fiction, magical realism, and utopian/dystopian fiction. It is a concept that I have long felt reluctant to identify within my writing as so much of my work is drawn from personal experience and therefore can also be categorized as creative nonfiction. In many ways, Armen Ohanian's writing was creative nonfiction, but as she wrote almost exclusively in memoir format, the speculation happened in a positioning that involved looking back. The speculative, for me, is tied with the concept of futurity. Mainstream narratives and ideologies tell me that queer motherhood is a contradiction—that bringing life and spirit into the world and caring for children are acts reserved exclusively for straight people in straight relationships. The speculation of how I might queer motherhood is absolutely a question of futurity here, then.

So my thoughts intersect around queer motherhood as an act of resistance and a fundamental aspect of my own practice towards queer futurity. I have often thought of queer motherhood as *speculative (non) fiction* - a reference to my own instinctual state of being as a mother as a constant act of *speculation*, of an immediate or faraway future, the speculation of which is fictional (or imaginal) because it has not yet come to be (but surely will, somehow). In many ways, as Muñoz argues that "queerness is not yet here" (1), for me, neither is motherhood, because it is always happening and never complete, and in the grander scheme of things, it is forever iterative and cyclical. The arrow of time and the circle of time have revealed themselves to me, congruently. The linearity of coloniality continues to disrupt my conception of time and futurity, and motherhood brought this disruption (back) into focus; it healed the wound but not gently, like surgery with no anesthetic, or whiskey on a bullet wound.

> *When they pushed their way into this world, a portal ripped my body open and remained that way for many months. During labour, the midwife kept measuring the size of this opening. As the numbers seemed to be increasing, I became worried that this portal would sever waist from hips, a magic trick gone wrong. There was a period of silence and bliss, in which my understanding of where the room ended and my body vanished entirely, followed by convulsions, an exorcism. Then she said, "ten centimetres," and I knew it was done growing. I did not realize until that moment that my experience of time and space had transformed; my perspective was no longer three-dimensional. My mother sat in the corner with smudged mascara, her mother whisper-prayed with eyes shut. I blinked, and this changed. They were weaving a delicate blanket of needlelace that stretched across floor and ceiling. A thin, dotted line glowed, no, sparkled, and made its way from the blanket to a nightgown that hovered above our heads. It looked familiar. It was unravelling from the bottom, disappearing quickly, row by row celestial thread being pulled at a frazzled pace towards another garment that was harder to make out. It could have been a bonnet. It could have been anything. It could have also been unravelling in the direction of the portal opening.*
>
> *This vision shattered into dust just as Saana released their first song onto my breast, a screeching symphony that still echoes through waist and hips.*

This memory above is crucial in my maternal myth-(un)making process—one that I have picked apart, interpreted, replayed, dreamed, written, talked, and thought about, obsessed over for many months. In many ways, and mostly inside my own thoughts, I have been processing my own version of autohistoria-teoría. Gloria Anzaldúa's writing encouraged me to imagine ways to "make knowledge, meaning, and identity through self-inscription" (6). Autohistoria-teoría is how I approach my understanding of moments like the one above, as it cultivates a space of remembering and future visioning that allows for a fusion between personal experience and theory.

And so, why is the moment above so important?

Until this moment, my worldview was fragmented like a herd of prey. Divided, conquered.

Only until I reach the moment(s) above, when gravity is lost in my being, when I have been ripped apart, fragmented, only then do I fully come to perceive the always both-ness of it all. A circle with no parameter, a womb within a womb, a mise-en-abyme, an image within image, a Russian doll. And what I have been struggling with is a restoration of the fragmentation caused by this imposed western Philosophical binary. Of course, Anzaldúa has been a strong influence here, as her writing was where I originally fell in love with the possibility of a restoration of both-ness.

There have been times since I experienced this moment, usually after reading too much academic literature that sounds more intellectual than I am meant to feel, that I have almost understood this as a colonization of my heart-mind-being. There have also been times, usually after too much medicine (depending on the strain) has flowed into my bloodstream, that I am able to return to the state of mind that I was in, during labour, when the portal opened (and there was both-ness) and never really closed.

All sense of my-self/being writhed in a prison of ever-stretching flesh from the moment they chose me as womb and caregiver. Yes, it was a choice—one made from whatever place that nonbeings exist, and they look down at us like a litter of kittens and say, "Oh, look at the one squealing in the corner. She's cute. I'll take that one." I am enslaved to this new creature, who is to become like me, a breathing, living being also, who I am meant to care for and chaperone through this temporal existence. I am a bodyguard. I am a risk assessment analyst. I scan their surroundings and evaluate possibilities of harm. I am the terminator. I would die for them.

I have died for them. In other lives that I am privy to since the portal opened. In my dreams, I speak to the mothers who died, and the mothers who lost them, who will lose them. Many mothers kiss my eyes, and I kiss theirs. In my nightmares, Saana is screaming ferociously, covered in blood, falling into endless pits, getting shot, being ripped out of my arms. Every time they come close to death, which feels as frequent as blinking, I feel the pain of a mourning-mother-version-of-me from another timeline. I imagine their death frequently, drawn to what I now fear the most. They are mostly horrific, violent deaths that come to me in waves or out of the blue. There is a gallery, no, a mosaic of images of Saana's demise in the depths of my mind that form a larger image even more dreadful than a thousand deaths. The image is a gaussian blur, out-of-focus, but I can feel it looming over me like a colossal statue of a nameless saint with secrets, laughing hysterically and crying blood tears.

They mix with my milk tears.

I have not bled in eighteen months.

Blood did not make me a woman. History made me a woman. Now I am woman no more. The skin of a mother slipped onto me in the night while I slept in a room with no light and now, as I crack crumble snap under the pressure of all this feminized labour, this, minutiae of mothering.

My experience of writing this is synonymous with new motherhood. It is defined by fragmented time/flow, interrupted sleep/thought, construction, collapse, infinitely breaking off, and starting again. I will start again here on one of the aspects of how we (those involved in Saana's caregiving) are enacting gender-creative parenting. We do this by intentionally facilitating an environment and relationships that will allow Saana to arrive at their own understanding and expression of gender. It seems radical, outlandish, and, to some folks, downright offensive. It is not a new or novel idea. Gender fluidity exists (culturally and socially) in various parts of the world.

It hit me during pregnancy. Folks kept asking my unborn baby's gender—never their sex— and often with an oversimplified dichotomous setup of "boy or girl?" Although I understand the sociocultural and political roots of this question, it pretty explicitly assumes both gender and sex as binary as opposed to a spectrum. And, inclusive of that, it also struck me as peculiar that this was asked of me. It assumes that I am a fortune teller. No one asks what my baby's favourite colour might be or what vocation they will aspire towards. Exactly as in their gender, I simply do not know the answer to those questions. And I realize that my choice is the result of my particular positionality. The way my worldview and family dynamics are queered is part of how I resist dominant (violent) colonial and patriarchal ideologies of gender pervasive in the West (where I grew up) as well as within my cultural community. I am reminded of queer scholar Jane Ward who refers to José Muñoz's focus on hope and futurity for queers of colour in *Cruising Utopia*. Ward links the potential of queer parenting to Muñoz's call for queers to "embrace projects that plant the seeds for a radically expanded future" (Ward 235). It becomes an expression of "desire for a thing, or a way, that is not here but is nonetheless desirable, something worth striving for" (Muñoz 121).

For these reasons, it is important to explicitly name that my gender-creative parenting is rooted in my own conception of futurity and my experiences as a queer, and diasporic-SWANA mother who was raised as woman. It is not for everyone. There are an infinite number of ways to parent—all rooted in experiences, positionalities, and cultural/social practices specific to each family. You do not have to understand or embody it, but you can respect it. A stranger crosses paths with Saana and me.

"Oh, so cute!" then turning to me, "Is it a boy or a girl?"

I reply, "They are a person!" smiling politely (the gentlest way I can respond, at this point in my life-learning).

Response 1: "Yes! Thanks for the reminder."

Response 2: "Um," they're speechless, nervous, offended. Discomfort is a great teacher.

A straightforward question such as "Is it a boy or a girl" is profoundly loaded. Moments like this have the potential to perpetuate particular ideologies of gender—how one must instill gender into their children, and how parents are in a particular position to perpetuate the status quo of gender (or not) and the power dynamics involved as such. My response ("they are a person") is what I have come to recognize as a micro-resistance—an explicit interruption of dominant conceptions and performance of gender as well as an acknowledgment and refusal to allow micro-currents of power as they relate to gender determine the docility of my body. In many ways, I have been thinking recently, it is not just a micro-resistance either. It is macro in the sense that power as it relates to gender is pervasive and problematic, existing beyond the confines of my family and community. Social transactions between caregivers and others—whether it is other family members, friends, or strangers on the street—are veins through which coded directives are being communicated; they ensure that we as caregivers are going to do our duty in upholding the status quo of gender in how we bring up our children and keep them in check. And these interactions are also sites wherein this status quo can be resisted.

I stepped into my maternal being in the early days of pregnancy with similar thinking as feminist scholar Sara Ruddick, who famously writes: "To claim a maternal identity is not to make an empirical generalization but to engage in a political act" (56). My process and transition of becoming a mother marked the convergence of what had long seemed fragmented and incompatible: my queerness and feminism, and my diasporic-SWANA lineage. This foregrounded a sense of futurity for me as descendant, caregiver for descendent, future ancestor—a fractal process reflected into/onto my work as a scholar, artist, and mother.

> *This is the first time, the first place that I will identify as genderqueer. Here, on this page.*
>
> *Becoming pregnant has been the queerest experience for me to date. Being brown and queer was a pull in opposite directions, a living in between two worlds. Becoming a mother was the big bang, not a theory—very fucking real. It fragmented my orientation and existence into infinite shrapnel. My intellectual understanding of dualism as a construction became embodied knowledge, and there was no other way to be/see/exist but in/as non-binary. My body became home to another consciousness, and all others before-after me.*
>
> *Ancestor, spirit, land.*
>
> *Can a mother identify as genderqueer after performing the most (historically) feminine act (birth)? My hope was to elaborate on it, here,*

but this is not actually possible. Elaboration requires a stretch of time to contemplate, a sitting with. I have no moments. I have a baby.

I believe that the disruption of my bleeding cycle during and after my pregnancy has halted the bodily rhythm that had given me a sense of time, a compass of time. And because it is a body sense, a body that is (sort of?) biologically female, not bleeding has stopped time for me. This absence of rhythm has impacted me in two very significant ways: It changed my perception of time, and it changed my perception of my gender. I think of how transformation of the world around us requires a transformation within. Gender creative, gender nonconforming—it's a family affair.

My intellectual and critical understanding of gender has become even more complex (and suspicious) since I became a mother and since I began to identify as genderqueer/non-binary. In a nutshell, I realize that the endless minutiae of mothering and caregiving is hyper(in)visible. When I speak of motherhood's hardships and challenges with my grandmother, she reminds me that this is the way things go and that "motherhood is sacrifice." I notice that since I had Saana, I feel ill when people tell me that I am a beautiful woman. So much of my struggle throughout matrescence is connected to how I am (seemingly) a woman-as-mother—the notion that my womanhood has somehow inevitably led me to my motherhood. This is how I arrived at not identifying as a woman, and this is when I began liberating myself from binary conceptions of gender and all its trickery.

Xhercis Mendez writes of gender as historically reconstituted and racialized throughout colonial relations of power. Mendez refers to Maria Lugones's colonial/modern gender system, which claims that the colonization of the Americas "introduced many genders and gender itself as a colonial concept and mode of organization of relations of production, property relations, of cosmologies and ways of knowing" (186). Mendez continues: "How we understand 'gender' makes a difference not only for how we frame our contemporary relations, but also for what we will consider to be necessary ingredients for re-imagining our various communities in liberatory ways" (55). This lands like a truckload of gravel in my already muddled pool of thoughts. Saana has woken; this is as far as I can go for now.

Motherhood—an alien invasion of every aspect of my life, my body, and my relationships. It's a good day if they wake me up with wet kisses. It's a good day if I remember to ask my partner about his day. It's a good day if I remember to breathe.

Breathing deeply, taking one full breath in and exhaling one full breath out without interruption or distraction is an act from a past life. Thinking is a luxury. I only have time to act. I am a body. I am outside my body. Motherhood is an outer body experience. I observe Saana; they observe me. I slip into their eyes. My eyes are not mine. They are my mother's and her mother's, and hers and hers and hers.

This rug is red, yellow, black, and old. It is magic, and it is hers. This magic is hers, theirs, ours.

Saana crawls away from me, turns back to make sure I haven't left (still here), and moves on. The space between us grows slightly, and in this space, time travel becomes possible. In this space, we are both making and inside memories past and future. They have seen past and future, accepted me for all that I was and will become: good mother, bad mother, and dancing mother. We are stars plugged into a constellation that connects us to generations past, to our ancestors. Every memory read and imprinted from/onto our DNA is a tiny, blazing ball of fire. This rug is on fire.

I am on fire. While Saana is busy fiddling with the tuner on the radio.

Little finger flicking through stations while snippets of word and song blow past our ears, echoing the symphony of unfinished thoughts that trickle into my head on the daily. My mind is full of emails I'll forget to write, groceries I'll remember we needed only after leaving the store, poetry unpublished. This is an inheritance; the skin of many mothers is weaved into mine. They whisper to me through the white noise of unclaimed FM, remind me of the things that slip through the portal cracks as I crack open and ash floats up and settles on the rug, they sweep, and tend to my burns. Many mothers tend my fire. The skin under my skin is always on fire. I am woman no more. The ways that I embody and experience time and space have been queered, forever. I live in a mise-en-abyme. Being within being, the never-ending-Russian-doll-effect. A multidimensional, timeless place that is also, paradoxically, tethered to the inevitable mortality of now. To their mortality and to mine.

Another (micro)resistance as a mother has been to acknowledge the simultaneous, pluritemporalities that I exist in/with. I experience time in multiple ways. My experience of motherhood has been embedded with this perpetual state of being anywhere between one and one thousand steps ahead of my child—a constant state of contemplative futurity. And the realities of being with my child have encouraged me to also be present. Saana lives in the present. If I want to be in relationship with them, I must also be in the present. Here is where the split occurs. I have to be both present and a step(s) ahead at the same time or, rather, have an awareness of both. In many ways, experience has fallen in line with both my queerness and diasporic identity (being both-ness). It has supported a new orientation for me because if I am either present in the moment or contemplating future exclusively, one or both of us will pay for it in some way.

> *This rug is red, yellow, black, old, magic, burning. It is made of the skin of many-mothers. So are the walls of this portal. It is smeared with ash and sunlight. It is soaked with their tears and my milk. It is stained with the blood that will soon flow, I hope, that the portal closes in on itself and I am freed. And again it comes to me, this time a whisper from the lips of many-mothers: Queer motherhood is speculative (non) fiction.*

Endnotes

1. An alternative to colonial and more commonly used terms (such as Middle East) in referring to a diverse geographical region.
2. The pieces of prose scattered throughout this chapter have been previously published in a different iteration. The citation for this publication is in the work cited.

Works Cited

Abrahamian, Kamee. "Queer Motherhood is Speculative Fiction." *Mizna [Queer + Trans Voices]*, vol. 21, no. 1, 2020, pp. 53-56.

Anzaldúa, Gloria. *Light in the Dark/Luz En Lo Oscuro: Rewriting Identity, Spirituality, Reality*, edited by AnaLouise Keating, Duke University Press, 2015.

Gumbs, Alexis Pauline, et al. *Revolutionary Mothering: Love on the Front Lines.* PM Press, 2016.

Jackson, Alecia Youngblood. "Rhizovocality." *International Journal of Qualitative Studies in Education*, vol. 16, no. 5, 2003, pp. 693-710.

Lorde, Audre. *Zami: A New Spelling of My Name.* Crossing Press, 1982.

Lugones, María. "Heterosexualism and the Colonial/Modern Gender System." *Hypatia*, vol. 22, no. 1, 2007, pp. 186-219.

Mendez, Xhercis. "Notes Toward a Decolonial Feminist Methodology: The Race/Gender Matrix Revisited." *Trans-Scripts*, vol. 5, 2015, pp. 41-59.

Muñoz, José Esteban. *Cruising Utopia: The Then and There of Queer Futurity.* New York University Press, 2009.

Ohanian, Armen. *The Dancer of Shamakha.* Jonathan Cape, 1922.

Ruddick, Sara. *Maternal Thinking: Toward a Politics of Peace.* Beacon Press, 2002.

Sacks, Alexandra. "The Birth of a Mother." *New York Times.* 8 May 2017, www.nytimes.com/2017/05/08/well/family/the-birth-of-a-mother.html. Accessed 17 Oct. 2021.

Ward, Jane. "Radical Experiments Involving Innocent Children: Locating Parenthood in Queer Utopia." *A Critical Inquiry into Queer Utopias*, edited by Angela Jones, Palgrave Press, 2013, pp. 231-44.

Chapter 4

Parenting (Selves)

Viridian Fen

1.

Incubating a child was one of the most alien experiences of all.

2.

Pregnancy was a wormhole,
Not a stable passage for travel back and forth,
But a nine-month hurtling one-way trip,
Into a different quadrant altogether.
Many of my automated systems broke down during the long months.

3.

What would it have been like?
To gestate and birth a child,
Already knowing in my bones,
Ligaments,
Uterus,
Vocabulary,
That I am not a woman.
That I am trans,
Sweet pretransition,
Confused femme-presenting me,
Role confusion,
Vague aversion to all the words for "mom."

4.

To be fair, it was true, like I had been told.
Pregnancy was an incredible mysterious delight unlike anything else I have embodied.
I read the books and had seen the videos. Marvelled at bellies and newborns.
Always expected to be a parent.
But. This? Is how humans typically produce offspring?
How bizarre.
What terrifying magic that with very little effort on my part,
the body I barely knew how to inhabit was hosting a new being.

I was expecting.
Expecting cozy moments of maternal connection,
not expecting the sense of physically hosting an adorable parasite for most of a year.
I wasn't expecting what it meant to provide them 24/7 nourishment, comfort, stimulation, and guidance for years to come in all matters of life mundane and awesome regardless of expertise.

I wasn't anticipating how the reality of my body would no longer make sense. I didn't know what dysphoria was. Growth spurt, even more invasive than puberty. Back then, I had learned comprehensive disassociation techniques. Now disconnecting from the humanness of my body and the other body it was growing was impossible. It became increasingly difficult to be okay with femaleness as pregnancy advanced.

5.

Confusion.
So little societal divergence ever glimpsed.
Gay femmes. Butch lesbians. Trans men and trans women.
No inkling of non-binary,
Genderqueer,
Everything else that exists.
Just the confusing uncomfortable wordless sensations,
Living in my body every day.

6.

I learned to perceive and traverse internal landscape while my body was changing in uncomfortable ways. Around my third trimester, I was taking excellent care of my body, but I could no longer connect to it outside of the necessities of pregnancy and labour. At the same time, I was beginning the unravelling of everything I had ever had a grasp on—myself, sex, gender, body, parenting, family systems, faith, the meaning of life, personal autonomy. I surveyed the spread of tangled fragments in front of me. My own experience of being parented was useless except for reference of what not to do. Confusing, mysterious, complex, layered incubation.

7.

(My mother is a ghost who used to be a witch. My father is a zombie who used to be a hippie. I myself was a changeling baby from another dimension who ended up with them by accident. How does one gestate and birth and raise a human youngling appropriately?)

8.

At the end of pregnancy, birth occurs.
In the clear otherworldly moment when birthing took control,
I could feel all the cumulative knowledge in the biology of the human body I inhabited.
It felt simple to allow it. Birth takes what it requires.
Scooped my child up out of the water.
Here you are.

9.

Transition of pregnant to parent.
The first year is hard, they say.

10.

"Please come," my mother begged.

Short months after birth,
Barely through yet another,
Longer,
Wrenching bout of searing infection related to breastfeeding,
We travel to another state for the holidays.

I tried to be normal and enjoy my family and show off my baby.
Holiday smiles and food and gathering together.
I cried in my sisters' tub, horror at all of us pretending to be normal.
Having a breakdown without knowing the word for it.

11.

Complex trauma
Abuse
Neglect
Perpetuated by my parents
Kicking me in the gut
Split me right open
Unspooling and spilling me into my bath water.

12.

The dysfunction was astounding in wide destructive mirroring ripples.
Nothing I knew about being parented or parenting could be used in my
own experience as a parent. Meanwhile, there was still a tiny person
relying on my body and attention and energy for survival.

13.

My trauma fully activated,
I was unable to breathe,
All I could do was breathe.
Learn to breathe underwater,
From the bottom of the lake.

14.

One night not long after that holiday trip,
I asked my partner to take our baby and leave the house for the evening.
Quiet,
Alone.
A rare moment for a postpartum breastfeeding parent.

I sat alone that night and cried for the anger and hurt and abuse,
For the horrible dysfunction I had just revisited,
my past child-self who had been utterly alone,
For the gaping holes in my development,
for my current self who had to figure out how to parent a child.
I cried and waited.
There, in the quiet and alone, after a long time,

.

.

.

.

No one came.
Nothing happened.

There was no presence of warm divinity,
Or some spark of inspiration or enlightenment,
Or angelic support or any thing or anyone.

Just me. Past me. Present me. Future me.
Just us then.
I got up. Washed my face. Drank a glass of water.
Okay. I will parent us both. All of us.

15.

After my night alone and realizing it was up to me save myself, to reparent myself so I could parent my child, I started trying things. All kinds of things. I realized I knew nothing and started there. Knowing that is something, as it turns out.

There were stacks of self-help books with cringe-worthy titles. I skimmed them for highlights and insights. I tried out different modalities of healing and development and therapy. The first time I went for energy work the practitioner told me I badly needed grounding, and I distinctly remember asking with total ignorance, "What does that mean?"

My functionality during this time was hard-maintained and limited to a certain number of endeavours. Anything beyond the capability of my remaining automated systems would send me into error mode.

16.

In the small spaces after a wave,
Before the next begins to approach,
I work out tiny pieces of logic.

17.

Mirroring my baby, myself, supporting our development as gently and fiercely as I could from wherever I was. Nervous system on the outside without my new skin grown over fully yet. Translucent and raw. Skin-to-skin contact with this tiny creature I had incubated. Giving birth had initiated such visceral, physical, structural, hormonal, mental, emotional, metamorphosis (transition). I wasn't able to operate the old system anymore. The next several years, I continued the work of that postpartum bath breakdown, pulling out my guts, wiring, old pathways, systems, the visceral idea of unraveling was persistent.

18.

Sitting with the enormity of the systemic trauma of my family of origin was overwhelming. I had just been back home, and they all pretended it was fine, that we never went through years of extreme religious and ideological isolation together and that the older generation never perpetuated all kinds of abuse, neglect, and perversion of development upon all of us who came after them.

Now I was a parent. What would I assign my child? What was underneath my skillful ability to rise to the expectations society had for my assignment? What if I stopped prioritizing those assignments at all? Who would my child be if I assigned as little as possible? No one who lives in society lives outside of its norms altogether, even if it is only being observed regularly by others through the lens of those norms. But what might it be like to grow up having even some societal expectations decentralized in favour of personal development? What could it be like for a person who grows up fully themselves and does not have to remove things like layers of maladaptive trauma responses and heavy-handed gender assignments first? What would it be like to be parented?

19.

To not be my family would mean unbecoming them.
Eventually, I wouldn't be one of them at all. Evolution.

20.

Microevolution.
Social evolution.
Personal evolution.
Social transition.
Personal transition.
Transition from non-parent to parent.
There are so many facets to being a human
So many sources of suffering
Surely SOME of them must be able to be removed or made less?
What might that be like?

21.

First, establish a healthy parent within myself.
Start with the basics of taking care of my own developmental needs,
With patience, perseverance within linear time.

22.

Second, do trauma work in the multiverse outside of time.

23.

Beyond the binary means,
There is a BINARY,
A default starting point, culturally developed norm,
There is a way of looking at things,
Collecting and categorizing.

IS IT THIS...?
OR!!!....
IS IT THAT?
WHICH ONE?

We (non-binary people) experience beyond this and that in our bodies,
Is that terrifying?
Is it magic? Revolution? Birthright? Breaking systems? Human
     nature?

This OR this.
Yes. Those exist. What about everything else?

24.

Quiet, alone, I start understanding. I see my parents fade from memory.
I can let go. I don't have to forgive. I can inhabit a world without them.
None of it (gestures grandly at the past) happened for a reason.
There are infinite possible realities in which none of it happened like
this at all.
In this one because of permutation of chance, choice of self and others,
statistics, systemic societal deficiencies, chaos, mystery, evolutionary
stage, it happened like this.
That's all. These are the bones I was born with, the story points I was
assigned,
Made up of karma, mysteries, prior lives, or something I don't know to
name.

Eventually, I made contact with the first healthy parent I had known,
my future self. The work and perseverance between them and me were
overwhelming. But once contact had been made, they stayed in contact
the whole time. They never left me. They had always been there, they
are nonlinear. I had finally caught up.

25.

What does it mean to get comfortable?

26.

Developmental needs

Infancy	ASSIGNED	FEMALE
Toddlerhood	ASSIGNED	FEMALE
Preschool	ASSIGNED	FEMALE
Elementary school	ASSIGNED	FEMALE
Puberty	ASSIGNED	FEMALE
Adolescence	ASSIGNED	FEMALE
Teens	ASSIGNED	FEMALE
Young Adulthood	ASSIGNED	FEMALE
Marriage	ASSIGNED	FEMALE
Parenting	ASSIGNED	FEMALE >>>ERROR>>>>>>

27.

During each developmental stage I was assigned, it was not as a cute suggestion or a helpful etiquette tip but as a religious and moral imperative—"female." The time and energy that my caregivers and parents put into enforcing the ideologies of that binary, the time and energy I spent carefully integrating and performing their lessons were all misdirected. Remove, rewire. In another timeline, there is a version of me that was able to go through development with non-binary support, and it's comforting to know they exist. In this timeline, I go through do-it-yourself second puberty while I parent my young child. I sort through the tangles of tapes and wires and systems that fell apart years ago. I pull out wires that surprise me by still being connected to something.

28.

When I am with a group of women, they inevitably bring up their shared femaleness, experiences of growing up and of now and reveling in their woman-ness... I am unable to access that. I don't have any emotional connection to it. I didn't have a pubescent development that was relevant to my gender. I didn't know I was trans when I went through estrogen-based puberty. I just knew I was always uncomfortable. Without any information or language or representation, I had always been non-binary.

29.

Probably like me, you grew up without ever hearing the word "nonbinary."
Without community representation,
without dolls that were green or yellow,
or anything other than blue or pink,
without non-binary TV characters or pronouns.
Probably you were raised in a constantly enforced strictly binary society.
Social evolution, the gender revolution has happened in our lifetime.
SOCIAL EVOLUTION IS HAPPENING IN OUR LIFETIME.

30.

It wasn't that long ago—I was a teenager when the first email exchanges—were becoming a norm for the tech-savvy household. As a young adult, I didn't have a smartphone until well after my baby was born. I had no Instagram representation, Facebook, Google, culture of instant access to the sum of human knowledge and exploration, hashtags, queer trans gender nonconforming people to see. Glimpsing gender ambiguity in public was rare and subtle; it didn't give me the information I needed. I didn't understand. I knew I wasn't a man. Or a woman. I felt alien. There's a sense of painful, lonely mystery when you don't see anyone who looks like how you feel.

31.

What kind of parent would I have been, would I be now,
If I had already been developed, myself,
If I was not scrambling to develop parallel to my child?

32.

Anger
Grief
Sadness
That my parenting began with self-parenting,
That I was non-binary the whole time.
There is an ache in my body that I won't experience pregnancy,
Looking down on my flat chest and round belly,
Bonding with my newborn without ever breastfeeding once.
The sensation of how much suffering I went through because I didn't know.
Because I was pre-op.
Sweet pre-transition femme presenting past me.
Someday at the end of my life,
I will have been parenting myself most of my life.
That self, that version of me, future self I will be,
If I listen to them and allow them to parent me now,
Who will I become?
It's the only faith that makes sense to me.

33.

Zen teachers say the present moment can be its own secure attachment.
Parenting. Attachment styles. Present moment. Past trauma. Future self.
I gently, fiercely make space for my selves to develop to be non-binary.
I carefully, observantly support my child's right to live in the binary or
not.

34.

I learn secure attachment and experiment with getting comfortable
while I parent myself and my child. Parallel play. We've been doing
this for a good while now. We are developing within this colourful,
fabulous, and wonderful burst of representation available in our culture
now. I am part of that representation.

35.

I teach my child what it is to be alien.
What it is to be a changeling, a shapeshifter,
A time traveler in a world that acknowledges
The existence of the multiverse.
My child teaches me what it is to be human.

Chapter 5

Otherhood

Serena Lukas Bhandar

As night descends, I feed my two rats and then myself,
Put on some music,
Smoke a little weed,
and then crawl onto my bed to dilate.

When I was young, maybe six or seven, I distinctly recall a feeling of joy, of liberation when I realized that I would never face the pain of childbirth, that I had lucked out with the genital configuration I was born with. I had a low tolerance for pain in those days—all it took was a trip and fall, or slamming my finger in the door, for me to burst into tears. I was a clumsy and anxious kid, so I cried often.

When I began taking hormones, I learned that they would likely make my skin more sensitive, more susceptible to pain. I was in the middle of laser hair removal treatments as well at the time, and I dreaded the impact my estrogen pills would have on the incinerating, electrocuting pain of burning the hair follicles on my face. So I was surprised when the next session passed easily and without complaint. The pain was still there of course, but somehow it was more manageable.

For folks who have testes and seminal vesicles, taking testosterone blockers is generally a one-way trip to sterility. I decided not to freeze my sperm when I started because of the financial inaccessibility but also because I've never really wanted to have biological children. The reasons for this are many, and although some are situated in places of shame (I'm afraid of passing on a genetic predisposition for depression), others come from more altruistic places—at least at first glance. When I was in high school, I stumbled upon the website for the Voluntary Human Extinction Movement (VHEMT) and ended up doing a presentation for my social studies class on why we should all commit to not reproducing in order to save the environment. I was high off of seeing the movie *Avatar* eleven times and didn't feel quite human. I thought that pollution was a problem caused by others and the world would be better off rid of our endless pestilence. I was also knowingly gay, in the closet, and had assumed I would be the "cool uncle" rather than ever be a parent myself. A couple of days after the VHEMT presentation, a friend asked me if I really believed what I had said. I said yes and that I thought it was irresponsible to have kids rather than adopt.

If I could go back in time, I would slap my younger self.

(That was also the end of our friendship, by the way. I later learned that she was Mormon and wondered if perhaps she had had a crush on me.)

I lie back on the bed and think of an English guy I once knew.

The dilator is hard ceramic and thick, and there's no movement, so it doesn't quite work. But I think about some of the amazing sex I've had since my bottom surgery and how much more there'll be once lockdown lifts. I think about riding a guy without a condom or going to an orgy.

Throughout all the paperwork for vaginoplasty, there are several instances where the consent forms clearly spell out, again and again, that the surgery provides no reproductive capacity. The vagina the surgeon creates is solely for sex, and this is demonstrated, again and again, in the behaviours and discussions from that crocodilian surgeon (who will remain unnamed here) and through the vaginal depth test[1] he conducts when you're healed enough to begin dilating.

If I'm feeling especially bored lying there on my bed, I see if I can stretch the dilator further. The pain is manageable, perhaps even erotic for me, and although I sometimes worry that I'll push too hard and break through into my intestines, perhaps I subconsciously hope that if I push hard enough, the dilator will go somewhere else, somewhere unexpected. I once heard a story about a kid in a sex education class who asked if vaginas are entrances to outer space. Maybe, if I twisted just right, the dilator would unlock a keyhole leading to a uterus I never knew I had.

When I was young, maybe seven or eight, I started imagining the names I would give my children if I ever had them. I don't remember many of them now, but Jade was up there, alongside Rose. Oddly enough, I have two transfeminine friends with those names. Or perhaps it isn't odd, and that I instinctively, serendipitously, knew the common naming conventions of trans women, even back then.

When I think now about adopting a kid or being in a relationship with someone who has one, I sometimes, rarely, let myself imagine having a son who never inhabits any marginalized identities—a perfect cisgender child who I could raise to be the best possible ally to myself and others. Again, this ideation of creating a childhood, a life, free from the troubles of gender dysphoria or chronic mental illness, is so thoroughly rooted in my shame in having experienced both. And it's not like raising a cisgender and neurotypical kid is a cakewalk, either. In fact, I'd even suggest that helping a child unlearn the normative and internalized messages that often come with growing up with those privileges is a far harder task.

When I was young, maybe nineteen or twenty, I learned that reproductive justice meant not only allowing access to contraception and abortion but also allowing space and resources for folks to safely have children. Genocide was no longer theoretical; it was a lived experience that I saw in the stories of my Black and Indigenous friends and loved ones. Later, in my trans and non-binary communities, I saw a vast array of children who had learned to be adults, and adults who'd never had a childhood. There were some couples and individuals who had been able to carry their own children, but the only few transfeminine folks I knew who had kids had them before transitioning later in life, and they grappled with their own different demons because of it. I still don't know of any trans women who have successfully adopted.

When we were young,

And the world felt full,

Did we ever expect it would be this hard?

Gingerly, I withdraw the dilator and then step into the shower.

My body aches to be left empty, but I'm not exactly sure what will make it whole.

Endnotes

1. For more of this flavour, read Juno Roche's essay on bottom surgery and pleasure at bitchmedia.org/article/pleasureless-principle-anatomy and meditate on her timeless words: "I'm much deeper than my cunt."

Chapter 6

The Work of Assisted Reproductive Technology in the Age of Mechanical Reproduction

Sunny Nestler

1. Chelonioidea Chimera

Protected by my shell, I skim my flippers over the warm, sandy concrete. My nesting site is close, and I am honing in on it, as my mother did before me. I don't recognize anything specific, but the landscape feels familiar. I have returned to the shores of my birthplace to dig my own hole. My plan is to leave a large clutch of eggs on this shore, buried neatly in sand. If successful, I will return in three years to repeat the process. Each grain of sand rolls in a jagged path a little farther towards the sea behind my majestic, leathery flippers. I flex my strong pectoral muscles one at a time, lurching slowly and deliberately towards my nesting site. Neither trusting nor suspicious, I am following an ancient instinct.

Dragging my belly across the ground is distracting. I feel the sting of fifty injections tingling on my underside. I hear a voice remind me, "We don't put pressure on oversized ovaries." I'm fairly certain that I am lying on my back, that my hind flippers are up above me, strapped to some kind of metal armature. No, that can't be right. I have to flip back over. Twisting, folding, unfolding, and refolding my body—or is it all in my head? I try to remember how I got here, but my mind fights off the attempt at linear thinking. I drift deeper, counting backwards farther still.

Forgetting the shape and classification of my body, I breathe mechanically and finally let my cells go transgenic, towards something entirely human. The other members of the Chelonioidea family are gliding through seawater, towards the surface to sip air, and then descending to deeper waters to find food. Except for my newest family member, Clo, who is with me, for now. Leaving my eggs behind is not abandonment; it is a natural part of reproduction. Scientists have been saying for years that we are a special family, the Chelonioidea, deserving of concerted protection. We are in the same struggle, even though our family consists of multiple species, because we are endangered, and this is widely recognized.

What was it the nurse said right before we went to sleep? Something about taking the freight elevator to the surgical suite to avoid meeting the intended parents. We shuffle past a pile of full trash bags, around ten of them stacked up, smelling ripe. We are in blue hospital booties carrying someone else's legal property in our body. We try to pinpoint the moments in time when the most important egg is ours, then theirs, then hers. Letting go of fear, we let the earth's magnetic field tug us away from the sea current. We let the doctors and nurses focus so we don't have to.

We relax into our own confusion, multiple species intersecting— creating potential for a new organism. Roughly twenty minutes pass, in what humans call "real time" while we try to picture the possible outcomes of this strange harmony. Future and past start to converge into a single point with increasing speed, and we swim towards it.

2. Ultra Sounds

In a hospital bed, Clo opens their eyes and feels their eyelashes pull apart from one another, sticky and wet. They blink away the last haze of anaesthesia. The sheets underneath them are wet, too. They lift one of their upper extremities, peeling it off the white sheet, one cell at a time. They hear sharp, staccato sounds, like marbles falling on a tile floor. What was their flipper just moments ago, breaks apart, and they see a clear vision of a thousand baby turtles scattering towards the water, bouncing along to the glassy sounds. They start lifting their other front extremity, impossibly slowly, the speed of a turtle. They recall knowing for sure what consciousness feels like—heart beating at a comfortable sixty-eight bpm, breath moving between lungs and temperature-controlled air. They can tell the difference between a memory and a dream, obviously. The hand gains elevation. Clo is lying on their back again, finally. It's soft and fleshy, cold and damp. Feeling is coming back into the nerves and the memory of speech returns to them but without the recollection of how to control volume. Clo looks with wide eyes at their decidedly human hand, suspicious of its origin. It keeps lifting ever more slowly, without their permission, as the words, "HIGH FIVE" come shouting out of their mouth at the first person they see. They try awkwardly to make contact between their sweaty palm and the nurse's dry one. Loudly begging for the results, Clo tells her that they need to know the results of the egg count right now. She pulls her hand away gently and tells them it is not customary to announce it so loudly because it might upset the other patients, especially when it's a really impressive amount. I see her wink from my inconspicuous vantage point.

Clo feels a shiver race down their clammy back, looking around the recovery suite. There are eight other patients, presumably all egg donors as well. The patients sit quietly in the same kinds of bed as Clo, in various stages of consciousness. Clo looks out the row of windows and tries to remember the last time they were in two places at once and, unsurprisingly, comes up blank. The egg is over here, the sperm is over there, and no one can remember this happening in their own life. I understand of course because I don't remember hatching in my nesting area, yet I know I was there and can always find my way back.

It is 2012, and there is no network of egg donors, just a peerless and unknowable group of strangers. Something about the transactional nature of what just occurred seems unaccounted for, just beyond Clo's horizon of understanding. Now Clo seems to be in a room of peers, but they cannot connect. They are shushed by the nurse, then cleaned up and hurried into a cab.

With Clo gone, I use my flippers to propel my body all the way out the door unnoticed, and down a hallway that connects surgical suites and offices. The uneven fluorescent lighting hums a little tune to itself as medical staff hurry past me. I can't tuck my head into my shell like land turtles, but I do have other ways of hiding. The features I have developed over millions of years of evolution cannot be described in your language. The lifespan of your entire species is not even a single grain of sand in an hourglass compared to what we have seen. Less than a blink ago, we watched dinosaurs roam a magnificent supercontinent, all of us wondering out loud at the dawn of the first flowering plant! Uniting with a human isn't unprecedented just because Clo doesn't know it's happening. How do you think we have managed to survive so long?

I wait for the right moment to start moving again. I turn my head and curve my neck around the next door frame, pushing the door open slightly with the tip of my curved beak. I see a man alone in the room on the other side of the door. I watch him as he ejaculates into a cup, or some kind of medical version of a cup. Letting out a grunt, he fills the container up as far as he can. He screws the lid on tight and places the plastic vessel onto a shelf built into the wall. Above the shelf is a sliding door. He taps twice on the door, proudly, and a gloved hand appears. The hand takes the strange vessel and shuts the window promptly.

Receiving a monetary gift in exchange for donating eggs is not legal in Canada, but in the US, it is. According to Canadian law, no humans are allowed to "create a chimera, or transplant a chimera into either a human being or a non-human life form." In the US, it is easier to do so. According to the Craigslist ad that Clo found, one just needs to be under thirty years old, in this case Jewish, and willing to help a family who is part of the same diasporic population. A gift of $8,000 will be provided in exchange. It is not a scam. The money arrives in Clo's bank account later that day. The moment when humans make chimeras intentionally is still in the future, but that doesn't mean none exist. Discovery—that human myth of creating something from nothing—is merely an unveiling of one of nature's subtler processes.

I myself have skills and use processes that are undiscovered; in this case, my backup plan. I scrape away at the sand in my nesting area, but something is wrong with it. It's cold and grey. Towers and grids of asphalt cover my entire nesting site. I can't bury my eggs. I know you would say that it's wrong, or even diabolical, to inhabit someone else's mind space and to meld with their body without them knowing. I'm not saying what I am doing is easy; there are of course important differences between sea turtles and humans. Choosing a human without a fixed gender is strategic. You may not be aware of this, but sea turtles don't even have sex chromosomes. Instead, our sex is determined by the temperature of the eggs during incubation. This has been described by James Spotila, one of the humans who studies us:

> Eggs in the center of the nest are warmer and thus more likely to become females, while those on the edge of the clutch are cooler and more likely to become males. The first and last eggs to be laid, then, are more likely to become male sea turtles. Indeed, which way an egg bounces into the nest might determine its sex. Many studies have shown that the middle third of incubation is a critical time for sex determination. Two days of rain during this period can lower the temperature of the nest four to six degrees. Thus eggs that were on their way to becoming females can end up as males merely because of passing storms. (15).

Not long after this first deposit, the sea levels begin to rise. A salty mixture of ocean water and garbage spills through steel and glass slot canyons, flooding the streets and the subway tunnels. The whole university hospital building is evacuated, but our eggs are safe in a freezer on the fifth floor. A human egg's solo appearance is not that impressive to me, but my own clutch of over one hundred specimens cannot survive a high tide.

Hurricane Sandy surges through New York City from October 22 until November 2. On November 6, Clo looks at pictures online of the block where we left our eggs, and it is under water. The storm is ferocious, but it does pass. The members of our new anonymous family are lucky, and the eggs don't get washed away.

3. Fast Like a Dart

Neither I nor Clo knows who the intended parents are; we just know that they are a couple, and that they need an egg. The donor agency has an address in Florida; Clo is living in British Columbia, and the intended parents are near New York City, very close to my own nesting area. The lawyer who draws the contract between Clo and the couple has their practise in Chicago. The contract divides up amounts of money to correspond with each step of the process, all clearly outlined. Clo receives $500 on the day of the first hormone injections; this is what begins "the cycle." They get another $1,000 on the tenth day, and the remaining $6,500 is paid out as soon as the egg retrieval is complete. The contract is eighteen pages long, emphasizing that Clo has no legal relationship to any resulting offspring. The exact wording is that the purpose of the transaction is to "provide female genetic material for the Intended Parents."

The profile match takes only one week, and suddenly Clo's life is all blood work, quiet nurses, and then the stack of paper that will numerically assess their psychological ability to cope with the process of becoming a donor. Statements like "I sometimes hear voices" and "I am generally optimistic when meeting new people," which they have to agree or disagree with, will determine the applicant donor's fitness to participate in augmented evolution. Clo keeps lifting the pencil and putting it back down on the table, rubbing both ends of the pencil against the pages full of text. The words repeat and corroborate, designed to outsmart them in five hundred questions or less. Clo is in the corner of a waiting room, sequestered at a private desk. "Your arms look like pin cushions," I say, as loudly as possible for someone like me. Clo agrees strongly. The psychologist takes notes about every past trauma, hungrily noting moments when Clo had survived any kind of suffering. A nurse takes blood, which is then lab tested, to see if Clo is a Tay Sachs carrier. Then come the questions about sexuality, very factually, but never about gender, or species for that matter.

After the day-long assessment, Clo wanders over to their mother's old neighbourhood. Thousands of miles from the place they call home; they get face down on the ground. This is it— my big opportunity. The sound of traffic is coming west from First Avenue, and the ocean waves are hitting rocks in the East River. The soundwaves converge and overlap, reverberating between Clo's ears. Their own otherhood feels, for the first time, pleasantly congruent with their mother's motherhood. I prepare to unite with Clo, a third layer in this trifecta of progenitors.

My species has an armoured head; no predators or other animals can crack me open. Clo's species hardly has any protection by comparison; it is easy for me to penetrate their soft body and relatively roomy brain. I am glowing and flickering with anticipation. I can bioluminesce; my skin can change colour. In this moment, it is easy for me to know what Clo is thinking; as we get closer to our goal, my non-verbal communication senses get sharper. I mask myself, and invisibly to anyone, including Clo, I unify completely with their mind and body. Our connective tissues knit together, forming a network of overlapping slipknots from intricate neural fibers, thin and strong and flexible. Our collective vision expands and sharpens; my ability to see the shorter ultraviolet wavelengths combines with Clo's ability to perceive the longer, red frequencies. Our visions merge and come uniquely into focus; we are going to reproduce together.

I try to project a future in which I make sense to the offspring, in which I am a contributor to them. Someone else will be in charge of picking out clothes, providing for human needs. I can imagine each offspring on a cellular level, though. Clo and I both can. Somewhere between the first day of the cycle and the eighth week of gestation.

Humans walk by, upright, trading baby pictures on their phones. We are on our bellies now, and we close our eyes in unison. Fully conscious, we enter a waking dream. In the dream we swim, as piles of purple sea urchins pass beneath us, closer to the shore with the rolling of each wave. We look at them so closely that they become magnified, appearing to move so close to our faces that we can identify the variations in each pointy spine, see each particle of sea dust clinging to the roundish, hollow lumps that form their bodies.

The next day, after the assessment, Clo flies home, and returns to their studio. They are in grad school, studying art. They are working on a drawing process that mimics DNA mutation and replication by repeatedly drawing shapes until they morph and diverge, spawning surprising new generations. Clo cuts and pastes these drawings, assembles them into landscapes, and scrutinizes them for relatedness. The hand-drawn creatures are lumpy and awkward. Clo can't shake the feeling that they are not alone in their studio, but then they have always had a robust imagination.

Clo rereads biology texts from past studies, looking for anything that can help them understand their role in procreation. A brittle sticky note falls out of a book written by Clo's former teacher, Jane Maeinschein, with a sentence underlined. Jane writes of the moment in history when the mechanics of reproduction became clear to scientists: "It was the folding, unfolding, and refolding of material in different ways that caused embryos to develop from unformed clusters of cells into formed organisms." This relaxes Clo—the thought of being allowed to originate as a folding cluster rather than a boy or a girl. Taking out a fresh sheet of white paper, they draw a series of long, grey worms, folding and unfolding the paper to segment each tubelike body.

Normally, Clo stays lost in the world of thoughts and ideas, operating with a low vibration. Clo hides their own body in oversized clothes. They don't like when everyone is looking at them, and they certainly don't feel comfortable as a medical specimen, in stirrups or otherwise. They have found a way to be comfortable in their body much of the time; the occasional out-of-body experience provides an escape valve during stressful situations. It has taken them until their late twenties to accept the changes of maturation, and now their body is about to change again. Despite this, Clo feels a calm resolve since their decision to donate their eggs.

Every person who hears about Clo's egg donation has a strong opinion. They think Clo is doing it for money or altruism. Misunderstood, Clo withdraws deeper into their work. Leading up to the first ultrasound, the contrast between intention and perception builds with increasing intensity. In a sterile office, Clo learns about the procedure. The way the ovaries will swell to make room for the extra eggs—from almond to grapefruit sized. The needle will pass through the cervix and suction the ripe eggs from their nest, having been released for potential fertilization exactly twelve hours prior.

The cycle involves taking hormones. There are injections of Follistim, a synthetic follicle stimulating hormone, every day. It comes in a spring-loaded syringe. Clo is surprised by how easy it is to use. Anyone could do it. Just pinch an inch of belly fat, poke the needle straight in, press the trigger, release the pinch, and the skin slides right off the needle. The next shot is a small manual syringe, like an insulin needle, full of another follicle stimulating hormone called Menopur. It comes in two vials that have to be mixed together. Birth control pills are also required medication, to synch up their cycle with the intended mother, lining up both uteruses for the planned eclipse. Lastly, an androgen is injected daily, to prevent unplanned ovulation. When Clo can't figure out how to perfect their technique, their favourite nurse tells them to aim once and put the needle in fast, like throwing a dart.

For the second time now, Clo travels across the country. For over a week, they sit patiently in the blood-draw chair every day, waiting for hormone levels to signal to trigger ovulation. Their mind drifts, and they become a tree in spring, with heavy fruits swinging from branches in rough winds. Clo lets go of reality so easily now that they welcome me into their thoughts. Without a clear image of what the offspring will look like, Clo becomes fixated on the shape of the ultrasound image. Passively looking at shapes on the monochrome screen, Clo detaches from their emotions, more with each appointment. Questions are answered mechanically. The repetition and shifting shapes of distorted circles fan out, black on black.

4. Decode Switching

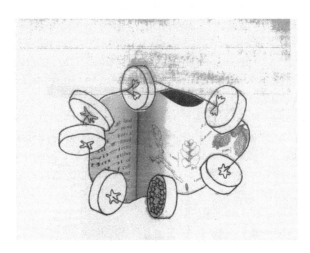

Our internal and external codes are always almost lining up. The code in our DNA and the codes we follow to participate in society are not much different from one another. They are written, and they are unwritten; they are hard to change, and they change all the time. If you wait long enough, they will change completely, and in one hundred more generations, they will be unrecognizable. Codes adapt, shaped by their surroundings. Two sides peel apart, make copies of themselves with the aid of special catalysts, and reform to spawn their next generation.

My own genetic materials peel apart and are remixed with Clo's. In a lab, they are then combined with the male parent's DNA. Intertwined with Clo under the sterile equipment, I push my egg concurrently into the aspirating needle. They don't know it is me, and that doesn't stop the procedure from working. A newer, shinier experiment will make everyone happy in the long run. Maternal, paternal, organismal, mother, father, other. Single celled egg, double celled egg. A beautiful fusion of commerce, industry, technology, and labour.

If you're thinking that I am a selfish shellfish, you are wrong on several counts; I'm not a bottom feeder. Clo gets to perform their own gender more precisely because of me, although they don't suspect me at all. Clo desires a structured overcompensation for their lack of maleness; they ultimately throw their seeds to the wind, little parachutes spanning out at obtuse angles to the horizon. Each plummeting seed forces a sunset on the era of one man, one woman, one baby. A collective pride settles over us both.

When the eggs are separated from our bodies, we separate from each other. Clo returns home and flops onto a heap of clean laundry. They lift up the bottom of their shirt and look at the tiny, faded needle scars, a few inches away from the spot where each ovary lives. They can see purple spines extending outwards from each point, magnetically changing direction, pointing towards me like compass needles. The particles of iron oxide in my nose light up and point back. My personal global positioning system detects magnetic input the way your eyes detect light; humans often don't know where they are, or where they're going, only the shape of what is directly in front of them. Clo drops their shirt and lies facedown on the floor. Their tears soak the carpet, a mixture of relief and sadness leaking out through the fog of familiar loneliness.

In the days and weeks after we decouple, Clo's dreams lose vibrancy. My voice recedes from their thoughts. They incorrectly think this is due to the familiar tide of hormones, amplified by a magnitude of twenty-three, one for each egg.

Satisfied, I slowly push my way back down to sea level. Saturated by the luxury of constant breathing, I am ready to float and to hold my breath. I am ready to leave this birthing place. With limbs splayed out, Clo contracts the muscles in their abdomen, pushing in response to strong uterine cramping. They breathe slowly, until a giant slug of blood crawls down their leg, twisting and writhing asexually, signalling the end of the cycle. The slug weighs in at twenty-three times the usual volume. Clo declares their first act of reproduction complete and falls asleep in their tears on the floor. A wave finds me now and carries me out to sea where I swim towards the current.

This is not the end of my and Clo's unusual pairing. Over the next five years, we reproduce two more times. One morning in 2017, Clo is lucid upon awakening and clear that the first of our eggs has hatched.

Three adult half-siblings intersect on a busy Brooklyn street corner, protected by only their backpacks. It is their first time meeting one another. Their invisible stamp of shared mechanical reproduction makes them feel calmly superior to the other pedestrians, as they walk towards the subway station silently. "Let's go to the beach?" one of them timidly suggests, following a strong instinct. The other two passengers nod and bob their heads in agreement. They sit facing each other on the train from Penn Station, studying one another's every feature. Matching sets of eyes, noses slightly curved into beaks. The year is 2035, and teens are still awkward with strangers. They clear their throats and look down at the green vinyl seats. They barely speak as they continue in transit, and eventually they are walking along the crowded shore. Limbs moving in asymmetric unison, they approach the water magnetically, not stopping until they float, eyes locked in a three-way stare. A shadow passes beneath them, about three-feet long, the outline of four flippers extending from an oblong body, rippling as the light refracts through the waves.

Works Cited

"Assisted Human Reproduction Act." *Justice Laws Website*. Government of Canada, 29 Nov. 2019, laws-lois.justice.gc.ca/eng/acts/a-13.4/. Accessed 18 Oct. 2021.

Maienschein, Jane. *Embryos under the Microscope: The Diverging Meanings of Life*. Harvard University Press, 2014.

Spotila, James R. *Sea Turtles: A Complete Guide to Their Biology, Behavior, and Conservation*. The Johns Hopkins University Press and Oakwood Arts, 2004.

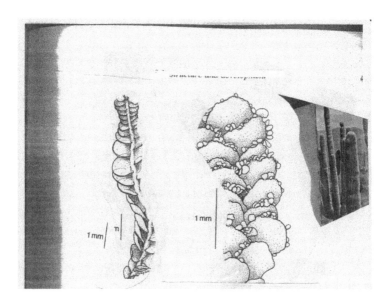

Chapter 7

Tales of My Infinite Chrysalis

Saige Whesch

If I could have spoken to myself when I had to speak up for myself, I'd say: "There is always something worth struggling for, and sometimes that's you—you are worth everything." But that's impossible. I'll tell you instead of my chrysalis moments. You will glimpse time as I do—in infinite layers and pockets. Of course, I have my tools and timetables in daily life, not to worry! (Purkis and Lawson). But through these chrysalis cross-sections of my transit so far, I plan to leave you with a richly composted, fertile hope about your own moments. Gender-exploring peer or ally, thank you for sharing time across these pages.

Part One: Egg

My name is Saige. It's a proud mix of my nickname and birth name that sits well.

As my mind sifts through these lived truths for you, I sit. I love a good seat. This one has solidly been there through books, two gestations, top surgery recovery, and one ongoing facial hair construction project. I suppose you could say I'm a bodybuilder of sorts.

Anyway, I and my chair rock my younger child to sleep. My husband gives quiet snores from between our older child and the cat, all who accepted me in all my forms. The baby breathes peacefully and taps at my ribs as I tap at the keyboard. This must be peacefulness. Words sizzle and rush, snuggling into place, finally, for who I am.

Identity is a multifaceted ember. It can burn, but it can also dazzle. At present, huge parts of this stolen land also burn (Faa). People in my home territory in so-called Australia face off against tropical drought, two words I'd never imagined together. Huge swathes of my body also burn, matching the weather pattern with surprising accuracy. A connective tissue disorder. Even with medical support, I'm still discovering what and how to adapt. Pain is purposeful when listened to and tells us what we must thrive beyond, be it the planet's pain or our own. My heart is both breaking and healing, in an emotional and a literal sense. It races under that weight. I find it uncanny the way my existence has melded with external events. My heart condition has always shown signs, just as my country has had signs of racism, misogyny, and dangerous levels of climate change for decades. And those are also best managed before damage becomes irrevocable. (McKenzie).

"When did you know you were __?" Psychiatrists, strangers, and even some who hold me dear have ended this question with a variety of labels. I only know that all matter and all matters of identity never remain static. I'm never completely knowledgeable, just sure enough for me. I never knew I was Trans, yet none of the other labels I was trying on (or forced to wear) fit correctly. Imagine being a caterpillar that can only live within a specific tree. You know there must be more to explore, yet you can't think of being comfortable because you're busy trying to survive, busy ignoring that warm shadow of eggshell heat still hanging over you.

Growing up, my family wasn't just a tree; it was an entire forest. The adults responsible for me and my sisters had friends and lovers who largely stayed connected. My parents parted before I was born. Knowing them now as an adult, I repeatedly thank them for that. They're so unalike! Yet they modelled a clear united front from multiple households. They informed me in age-appropriate ways about my eyesight and taught me how to be Disabled and proud in the face of stigmas or challenges. Drawing fortitude from the lessons of those who parented me, who nurture around me, I show compassion to my body, which continues to teach me to defy limitations and expectations from outside and within.

When I was ten years old, I didn't know that I was neurodiverse, or nonbinary, or really anything but the cis/het mold I saw forming around my future. But there were moments that shone—the euphoria beyond verbal language—of swimming through surf just in shorts, having ditched my shoulder-length hair (to deal with head lice), eliciting the new and sharp sensation of brine on my bare head. The unexpected freedom from conventional beauty and mannerisms, even temporary and so young, was one of the best gifts. But I didn't know.

I didn't know when I was even younger, cast by my peers in male social-play roles because of my lanky body—why I liked that my friends saw me as some kind of character chameleon. I only knew the fun of being Peter Pan, the danseur noble, Daddy Bear, or the cat's girlfriend. The playground supervisor would watch our games. I recall seeing them pick their jaw off the ground and ring the bell to return to the classroom.

One weekend outing, I recall a small group of girls around my age splitting off to play in an area away from the rough-and-tumbling rest of the pack. An angry grief rose in me. I wanted to be with the small group, but I also wanted to climb and be rough. I wanted playmates like me. Conflicted as I was in that moment, I can now name the feeling of not being feminine or masculine enough for either group at play. But at that development, I could not. I swung my way up the outside railings of the playground bridge as another child my age ran up the slide; my frustration and his flagrant rule-breaking made me lash out. As he reached the top of the slide, I swung from the bars and kicked him with both feet, knocking him off the playground. Sometimes we think we have the right reasons to act rough, I instantly realized that I did not. The boy was crying and had cuts across his hands from landing roughly on the woodchip base. The other children and adults glared at both of us—scorning a girl for being mean and a boy for showing weakness. Our mothers argued. Embarrassed but still defiant of my internal conflict, I claimed the slide as my domain and played alone. Regret and maturity came later, at the same time as I was in the middle of surviving domestic violence and shared trauma. So I kicked my budding gender identity aside, something I do not recommend to anyone.

"Did you always know you were nonbinary?" Not in so many sleepovers, bubble baths in the dark, unexplainable angst in public school health subjects, or being secretly delighted if another child asked if I was a boy or a girl, and I got to respond, "Does it matter?" No. But to that question, I'll offer another: When does anyone know who they are? It is not solely told to us or from us at any one moment, much as we puzzle otherwise.

Pervasive messaging told me that I was becoming a woman. *Strange,* I only answered in my mind. *I still feel like me! Why can't I say this out loud?* I didn't know why, at the age of fifteen, I found myself crying in the mirror at the strange yet familiar face going through adolescence. If only I'd known that sometimes people have more than one puberty. My ribs ached, my heart beat irregularly and too loudly from my suppressed sobs. Counselling has since shown me that I was developing depression, anxiety, and complex posttraumatic stress disorder, and they can all be appropriate survival responses—provided one survives to access appropriate, individualized healing.

So, there was this hatching me, looking in the mirror, not verbal and prodding at my plump, smooth cheeks, at bumps beneath my shirt, and running a hand through hair that felt foreign, too aware of the sensations. There, I was discovered. My mother made empathy a superpower, and even though she did not know what I was really facing, she knew to check on me, as only people who parent themselves and others tend to do. Only I couldn't fully express what was happening, beyond wanting to feel content with what and who I was and not being able to find that happiness. The sense that it was my reflection speaking intensified from then on. I thought "transgender" was a word for fictional characters and violent headlines, so I didn't mention it. I was just another teen dealing with growing up. A butterfly wouldn't realize there is anything beyond their chrysalis initially, either.

I didn't know. I thought it was perfectly alright to only go to the bathroom at home (an eight-hour marathon during school days); or to have a churning gut after eating anything not a soft plant; or to have to sit for a long time after playing sports, watching the pulse flush in your legs and counting blank spaces, the silver stars floating across your vision. These dysautonomic traits **could** have been due to my lifelong eye conditions; my living experience was always explained away as such at checkups, but that never quite felt right to me. And by then, I wasn't able to take my own instincts seriously. I believed I was like a sapling or a giraffe—of course a young person would be able to bend and stretch a little further than others during yoga. The Indian-Australian teacher tried to let me know to avoid overextending, but I wasn't very practiced or aware of subtle conversational or facial cues. His concern and warnings passed me by. I became detached, amused by everything my body felt. I pushed myself through the rest of my school years physically, mentally, and emotionally. I tried to just get on with life, as my woman ancestors had and trans ancestors had in secrecy. It's not actually very nourishing or safe to do that for a long time, though. But I was busy learning to support myself financially and emotionally.

It got busier. Somewhere therein, I agreed to be whatever people around me saw. A girl? Alright, sure, as long as nobody gets hurt. But I was hurting due to what I now know are my disabilities, and I was ignoring the pain due to the medical authority figures advising that was the best decision. I was also daydreaming that one day I would just wake up and know who I really was, that I'd stop feeling like I always had to put on a costume and mask to be respected and accepted.

During these formative years, I kept a small group of friends. Every single one of us is now out and learning that special, quiet pride and acceptance. We're all gender flavourful. Some have discovered intersex histories; some of us are ethically nonmonogamist, ace, or some combination. As we age, we all have had disability, neurodiversity, and chronic illness shade our experiences. None of us mentioned any of these during school, yet we are supportive of one another, as we each work to reshape what we have internalized and work to determine which messages are worth holding onto.

Part Two: Growth

During that time, I didn't realize what I had internalized. But I did get to know the friend who nicknamed me "Sai." Aaron was the person who I'd eventually date, share a house with, and later marry. I started learning to sift my thoughts and cope with scarring memories. In a quieter town, at the opposite end of this large continent from where either of us grew up, he showed me a scar on his hand and told me a story of being kicked onto some woodchips as a child.

"Oh, ow. Wait. Um. Was this at... er," I stammer on, detailing the place. He filled in accurate details where I left off. "Yes, the slide was yellow, shaped like this?" He moves mesmerizing hands to describe it. I might have caught feelings. "In that case, I think I owe you an apology." I confess. "Seriously, that was you?!" Is he going to be mad with me? That's justified but also oh no! I scrunched my fingers through the laces of my shoes as these thoughts raced. But Aaron was looking at me to respond.

"Yeh, I think I had a whi-"

"A white dress and blonde hair." He starts cackling. "Well done!"

"Wait, you're not mad?"

"No, that's impressive. You're still a strong person."

"But I was an asshole."

Together we determined not to employ any of the emotions from during that event as we built our adult relationship together. We did, however, laugh ourselves to the floor.

Just after we came home from what I call "a much needed avoidance of people" and what others might call a honeymoon, I was in a workplace training and experienced my first introductions and pronouns round.

"So. What does this mean exactly?" I interrupted. I used to do that a lot. "People use all kinds of personal pronouns to describe themselves and others." The facilitators were patient with me. "Like 'you,' 'us,' 'she,' 'he,' 'fae,' and more." This made me feel as though I could soar. "Sai, why don't you come and write what name and pronouns you'd like to go by in this space today?" Affirmed by the use of my at-the-time nickname, I stood, overwhelmed or just dizzy from the heat (or maybe because of my heart condition, too). Each step towards the whiteboard got easier. Shocked that character creation options beyond the assigned could exist outside a video game, I chose the bright red marker:

S A I G E — she/they

I tucked my wish on the end, letting that part of my identity remain attached to how I thought I should present at work. After a short pause, people around the room smiled, and then we moved on with the agenda of the day.

That night, I asked Aaron to help me explain some feelings to him. Over a meal, we learned some names for genders beyond the binary. He stressed that I would be me and he'd love that. I stressed that our love was already adaptive and flexible beyond words, that I had no idea how much I needed to explore, but he was welcome to discuss anything along the way. Our relationship and orientation were never linked to me coming out. "Sai, you know you don't need to worry about me. Or us." "But I am. I'm feeling unsure about a lot since today." I watched his still, tented hands and noticed his number of syllables: "We want to be together for, hopefully, the rest of our lives. We've said that so many times, right?" I was twenty-four and unable to respond. I wiped my tears, contemplating if I'd wiped his tears, too. I nodded too quick, and our teardrops merged on our smoky glass tabletop.

Something clicked in my neck, not painful, but I couldn't quite get my eyes to focus on his face. We leaned on each other's shoulders with easy familiarity. "Everyone," he steadied his breath and stroked my chin. "Everyone in long-term relationships won't be the same as they were when the relationship started, be it looks, attitudes, illness, fashion, or gender." These words brought irrefutable warmth as well as a sense of peace and security I thought I'd broken by coming out. These words remain as forty-one syllables embroidered in my memory—a soothing blanket for a ceaseless mind.

Part Three: Exoskeleton

"When placing a sleeping baby from your arms to the bed, it's important to make small, fluid movements and remember to use the power of the pelvic floor to take both their weight and yours." They should name a martial art after this. Oh, in a way, they have—it's called a "mothercraft" lesson. And that's about all that I remember from my hospital prenatal classes that isn't distressing. Placing them safely on their bedding, I watched deeper sleep flowing on, I remind myself that such classes are holding more space for more of us (groups like Birthing Beyond the Binary; Rainbow Families). These days, I avoid situations where filtering and translating cis-centric talk is demanded of me, unless I choose to take on that role. But I try and remember when I wasn't so privileged.

"Is this planned?"

It was just after Father's Day when we first found out I was gestating. I was tired from the previous weeks of the 2013 Australian Federal Election beat. I had my first paid contract in several years' worth of working and the far-right had come further into power as my activist life developed. I felt alright in the snug and sterile medical office, though. There's safety in invisibility. The nurse who was sitting opposite me smoothed out a piece of notepaper while our rapport crumpled. "It wasn't *not* planned." It's not an exact binary, this language stuff. I tried following up with a little smile to fill the pregnant pause. She'll never know I'd had to stop my birth control a month before we conceived. It was a trade-off between physical discomfort and deeper and longer states of depression. Aaron and I came to the mutual place of feeling comfortable enough to see what would happen without it. Privately, I thought that I had been born too prematurely for my systems to be so fertile and functional. I had felt ovarian and abdominal pain on and off since my menarche, and I'd given up mentioning it and managed it with home remedies and a ridiculous stubbornness I maintain to this day.

Having moved south to escape harsher weather events and rising living costs, these antenatal appointments happened in a hospital much like the one where, generations ago, a dominant morality meant that children born in unfavourable circumstances were forcibly put up for adoption, including some of my ancestors. This ideology is still perpetuated against First Nations and migrating families here to this day (McKenzie). I set this knowledge aside and followed the nurse's line of questioning. Our nurse very kindly and expertly checked my vitals, scoped out any potential partner violence as required by protocol, and tried to get to know me. It didn't even occur to me to be out and birthing until we were seven months along. By that point, I was losing the energy to conform to cisnormativity's expectations. As I cocooned another being's forming existence, I had to toughen myself, to show more of myself. I'll forever be thankful to my children and this body for bearing me through that.

One day, walking home from an utter treat of a pregnancy massage with an allied health practitioner who was polite enough to not care to use any pronouns or ask me small talk I still can't stand. I felt like I was floating. My employer had been understanding of my fatigue so far, finding auxiliary tasks and research to assign to me. The nausea was lessening, and I'd told my loved ones and friends beyond Aaron that I was nonbinary. Only after that did I choose whom to share the baby news with. Aaron trialed parental titles for me to hear—Mum, Papa, Ren, Zaza, Baba, MaD, and Sai— until we'd fixed on Papa Zazza. I must have had quite a spring in my step that day. I was wearing a skin-tight, zebra-patterned pregnancy dress, which was the most comfortable I could feel when required to wear clothing.

As I did my peppy waddle over the last street before home, a motor roared and transphobic slurs from its driver left me supporting myself on the side of a cheaply constructed block of flats. These were the same bricks from a recurring childhood dream, the kind where the dreamer is being chased. The last time I'd had this dream, I found a way out by picking up a coat that morphed my frame from adult with pear curves into a frame that was wiry, small, and masculine. I stopped running away from the chaser and instead ran, smiling, towards the exit. I realized that the dreamscape exterior happened to have the same pattern as the wall that I found myself supported by now. I connected this pattern of thought, grounding myself by running my fingers across my undercut hairstyle, and regrouped from my first waking violation of being yelled at just for displaying myself authentically. Then I got some mates over to cook a stir-fry. The rice was dry.

As that season's heat relented into rainfall, the baby's head was suddenly dropping lower than I thought possible. My femurs and pelvis slid in a few directions at once, more like a galaxy forming than anything dislocating. I didn't feel pain in those early birth-y moments. The federal budget had also suddenly dropped, with cuts to essential supports that affected everyone I knew directly, an all-too-common governmental practice in my experience. Mothers' Day was coming up, and mould had sprouted in our roof. I was very distracted.

We made a flexible birth plan because we didn't know any other people like us. There was no known library of autobiographical experience to draw empowerment from. The clear plan points were: *explain my options to me, use audio/verbal cues, keep bright lighting and scissors to a minimum.* I forgive myself because our situation was defying stereotypes and expectations. If only we'd had a hospital team where we weren't their first encounter of the Queercrip kind.

Midnight, not much later that autumn, we left a note on our rented home's door and passed on the key so our cats could be looked after. Soft internal knitting, which I thought were quickening Braxton-Hicks practice muscle surges, got terrific within me. Driving to the birth centre, Aaron and my father joined me for labour breath work and other mammalian baritones permitted by the traffic-induced tightening of a seatbelt. The night roster staff we hadn't managed to meet yet did their best with my physical wellbeing but fumbled to support anything else. I felt invisible and all-too-visible in my most primal moments—

threatened yet untouchable. And then I let out a howl in the face of an unwitting and unknown midwife, who'd been attempting to direct my sounds inwards. I wished that I was confined back in the car seat where I'd felt more welcome.

I let out a human baby. I felt like a fish when that fetal ejection reflex occurred. I was free from any With my particular neurodiverse, Queercrip, settler-descended voice, for an eternity wrapped in a single minute. Aaron's hand was at my side; his voice requesting and claiming whatever space for us he could. "Don't clamp the cord yet. They're both alri- no. Stop." I took a breath in and made some vocal mammal noise all at once. Humanity's first language, lost except in birth. Scissors, I felt the floor vibrate as they landed softly near my foot. This new child was then placed by the midwife doing her skilled thing, on my belly but this time on the air-facing side. "Don't. Clamp yet," purred my primary partner. I breathed out. Anchored to him and to her and to the newborn through gentle, loud touch. My heartbeat slowed and soothed me. I realized I had brushed my fingers on our umbilical cord. Our pulse felt strong. And then the baby opened that newborn voice and voided their bladder in a beautiful affirmation of existence and disgust.

Surrounded by too many nursing hands and long sentences, I curated the chestfeeding, nursing relationship between us two. It wasn't easy, but it wasn't a hard choice to keep trying. During those first few nursing days, the protests against the Coal Seam Gas fracking near Gloucester, New South Wales, reached a peak with a Mother's Day Breastfeeding circle sit in. Although I could not attend as I was healing from blood loss and a tear, I felt held by this online community of women activists. For the first time, it felt like it was okay that I was like them but not one of them.

"How amazing to be here on Mother's' Day! That's so sweet for you!" Rounds time in my hospital bed and, I had to assume, another under-the-pump nurse who hadn't had time to read my pronouns. I did my little smile and kept my head tilted towards our baby.

"Heh, yeh. You have no idea. It's unbelievable." Came my reply, as my neck did its now-familiar crackle. As soon as we were alone again, I pulled down my clothes and stretched my shoulders, which chimed in with more crackles, and settled the two of us for some skin to skin. I switched sides and dropped the nipple shield. Aaron was due back soon, but it was still frustrating enough that I heard myself swear: "Ah, titty sprinkles!"

We required some supplemental formula for a few weeks, and I do feel I must emphasize that each family's decisions are best for each family. I had signs of Raynaud's Syndrome, which is when the circulatory system acts like it's at the gym and one's skin becomes sensitive to even the slightest cold or pressure. I also developed inverted nipples. Supplement infant formula, appropriate lactation consultancy, nipple shields, and soft lupin heat packs were made for times like these. I used to think of travellers and warriors whenever it was late in the night as I gathered my courage to ask for help. "Husband, fetch my pack and shield!" His replies always made me smile—"Pfft. That's what she said." And when it was this particular reply, it soothed some of the sting from the misgendering that occurred in our otherwise supportive web of people.

As soon as I translated the advice and instruction from cispassing, able-bodied, neurotypical medical providers into something I could work with, we started to have our milky sessions by touch, smell, and sound. Finally able to get my milk out, I reached a lower level of pain, and we made it through towards the end of our first year, replacing formula tins with a budget for nutritious snacks for me. This snuggly lactation relationship and my new family evoked something powerful and primal that predates any social constraints. As accomplished and genderless as nursing felt, I began to wonder what a flat, sculpted chest would be like. For the first time since I was twelve years old, I went braless, which was excruciatingly great. Yet I still did not realize that a nonbinary person could engage in a physical transition—that anyone can craft elements from the physical, medical, legal, social, and whatever else they can access to affirm themselves. On the bright side, I found a community message board online and went stealth as another new mum. Although I didn't know what to call a vasospasm or know all the flavours of milk duct blockage, me and the baby, who we had named at five days old, found our nursing rhythm together with people from all over the country. I pumped extra, for comfort, and donated informally whenever possible. It wasn't strange to me; I'd been told of the milk donors who supported me as a premmie baby. I have been privileged to support two gay and breastfeeding community organizations and to add people like me into their circles of solidarity.

Producing any amount of comfort and milk directly from my chest made me proud of my mammal body, even though sometimes I set unattainable goals that I had to turn into new goals that were less difficult to achieve. I came to understand two things.

One, I found that pregnancy and postnatal times were like my experiences with chronic illness and disabilities. I found that a few friends will check in on you, mostly online. Two, each hour can be vastly different than the last, especially when there is a lot to feel and take care of. So, nothing I couldn't handle.

The first one thousand days of parenting life saw us move to another town, in yet another state. We couldn't afford to stay where we were. Thankfully, this time, we had a few friends to help us settle in. At the new part-time daycare, I was always scared of seeming like I was pushing some agenda when saying even little things like, "I'm called Papa Zazza, not Mum or Dad." I always added the "or Dad" part to help validate myself and try to take the pressure off the staff and my youngling, who soon adopted this phrasing and would beam brightly when correcting playmates. It was one of the room leaders who first told me of the Being, Belonging, and Becoming framework for early education and who connected my parenting moniker and relationship back to my child in a great way. That one small conversation helped me know how to talk with teachers, as we approached the primary school milestone. Out walking one autumn day, this happened:

"Hey Zaz, why don't I have a mum in my family? This one kid at kindy says I do, but I don't!"

Small feet stomped in teal dinosaur sneakers; I knew the clashing of developing understandings of the world. I had been preparing and dreading a moment like this. So, I took a slow breath and kept my walking pace even to show that this is normal and that discussions between child and caregiver are welcome.

"Well..." The L sound dragged on a bit too long. "Some people don't know this, but you do already. Some families have mums; some do not." I waited to see if there was more curiosity before going on.

There was. A smile from this young, already resilient child wiping her tears that had formed between frustration and gusts of dusty mountain wind. It had been another dry year. Grass crackled under our feet.

"Well, you have a daddy and a mummy," she told me. "So, it's not always the same." We would have continued this discussion, but we had to balance on a wall and blow on some dandelions.

The federal election that came around again allowed me to flood my mind with workplace patterns, expectations, and procedure. I couldn't stand nor stop the train of thoughts that sprung up around my gender and were developing in synergy with my little part of society, my young family, when I went to bed. So I stayed up later, got more done but felt emptier and emptier as the weeks elapsed faster. Did I find my community at local social events? No, they were all in times and places I couldn't access. Did I ask for access help from local disability services? No, I was already burned by having to be closeted for perinatal healthcare. At that point, I'd never heard of another Trans and Disabled person. So I delayed all the specialist appointments and social engagements I possibly could, often deferring to a vague reference of it being a school night, or at naptime, rather than begin to untangle what was really needed.

I did end up doing something for myself. I went and got an IUD to manage contraception and menstruation. It took two doctors. The first was unknowingly hurtful, and rather than educate with a face between my legs, I used my privilege of location and went to another doctor.

The future plot device lasted me a few months' very surprised gender dysphoria relief while I continued being Too Busy. Until the day I wore a vivid mascot suit for a job and the IUD slipped silently with a little of my hypermobile connective tissue. The doctor on duty was empathetic and had a straightforward way of telling me how I was healing and what my options were. My patient intake forms contained all the information about my pronouns and gender, so I thankfully didn't have to correct anyone. Just like during pregnancy, I was getting too tired and busy to not be out and, in my own quiet way, proud. My body taught me that contentment cannot come only from what I feed or medicate it with. Contentment has more to do with how I am in partnership with my body, how I claim my body with actions and creativity. I learned that I was okay with a more immediately reversible hormone replacement and begun reading anecdotes and health journal pieces on testosterone and blocker medicines. Having supported me through my own health efforts, Aaron followed up on some of his ongoing symptoms. He was found to be completely healthy but with a healthy dose of arthritis.

Living through Australia's Marriage Equality Plebiscite, we tried to find our strength and resolve as in community and individually. So I edged painstakingly across the fringes of this public debate. Like many Intersex people and gender varying folks impacted but not often included, I navigated kept gates to legally change my name and passed one year of elective bonus puberty with hormone therapy. The Plebiscite question and policy wording were argued over publicly for years. It was a small relief to see our child mostly protected from it. Mostly. Aaron and I were careful when and how we talked about it with anyone. We carefully tone-policed ourselves waiting until naptime to watch the coverage on the news.

We joined a rally for equal love and were surrounded by swarming supporters, Queer ones and their dear ones, ducking and weaving with their rainbow flags. They used bright signs and song to block out the scared, hateful little group installed beside the merry-go-round. Itself a transported relic intended for light amusement only.

Not amusing at all, our marriage certificate remained valid only because I could not change my own birth documents without multiple sterilizing procedures. This put me between a rock and a hard place when the Plebiscite question came through the letterbox: "Should the law be changed to allow same-sex couples to marry?" Yes, of course, but so many of us still wondered how the law would understand our relationships to those we love. The local post box was covered in rainbow pride stickers. The little clap of envelopes landing on more envelopes was soft and final.

Again, it felt sudden Aaron got selected for some more long-term work in his desired field. A fortnight before the vitriolic, fearmongering public debate and vote results announcement, my own job contract began to wind up. Emotions were at a constant, closely watched simmer. A couple of chosen family mailed us glittery notes of encouragement. A silver lining when one was most needed.

During this leap from several underemployments and late night logistics, we moved deeper into the suburbs to remain sheltered as our rental home turned a profit for someone who boasted during the only time we met, about how many "properties" they owned. We posted our Plebiscite survey answers before we moved, and we left some of the confusion and hurt behind. We received a reply from one of our countless applications, not only were basic services and school now bussable, our new nest was also within the catchment for a homebirth program connected to a public hospital. I saw my opportunity, the stability of place and hearth. The yes vote won the marriage equality plebiscite, and the highest percentage of those yes votes came from our area. My cycle gave visible, roughly monthly red signs again.

To keep my doctor as an ally, I complied to a pregestation blood test. For what felt like the longest time, we charted, mixed all the necessary ingredients, and hoped for a second gestation to begin. I related to emus, seahorses, and penguins, who have shared in masculine-of-centre parenting roles as I completely distanced myself from any personal pronouns as often as possible. This time, I knew how to advocate and curate my support team, what papers were accepted with red pen additions, this time the outcomes were healthier than ever. I shelved identification document updates and formed a truce with my large chest. I wanted to see how much milk and nurturing I could do this time, with this new peace of mind, this acceptance that came not only from friends and many relatives but from within myself. I decided on a top surgery clinic in case I needed a lighthouse, but I expected that having learned to nurse with one infant, I could do it again for longer.

I still know the exact date and time that gestation started for us, although the current (Western, at time of writing) method is to date all pregnancies from the last known period (LMP). I celebrated with close friends and some ice cream despite lactose intolerance. It was one of those golden Gay times, obviously. It was a super-charged gestation period. It felt like this time it went by quickly. Yet went on an exceptionally long time. Surely, it's been forty weeks! My thoughts splashed around, while I sweated from morning-but-really-all-day sickness. It was week twelve, but I would feel nausea without having much to show for it all the way through to birthing.

I was listed as male at a government-rebated physiotherapy clinic. Male is what my doctor wrote on the referral letter, so I felt I had to let it slide. Everyone was being so caring and good at their jobs. I thought, *What if I make them confused, and they waste our session time asking for clarification? What if they tell me to go somewhere else?*

To avoid the inner storm further, I chose the level of stealth implied by the letter, leaning against someone else's labels for me. The Physio contacted my general doctor, I was later informed, instrumenal to developing a diagnosis for my bendiness and a management plan for my symptoms. She helped to reposition my hips and limbs, and then I would sit so carefully on the bus ride home so as not to redamage myself straight away.

One such afternoons, the preschool teacher seemed to smile a little longer when I arrived.

"We've been told someone's going to have a baby sibling!"

My hands darted to my beard and belly bump as I allowed return delight to surface, feeling temporarily in another dimension, welcomed, no judgment or need to debate my existence, or scramble to justify the histories of it all.

"Yep! We're excited to meet them when the time is right!" I breathed a little easier and listened about my child's day.

They made pancakes!

Part Four: Chrysalis

With the instability of paid work like a silk rug on a staircase, we needed to access welfare support for part of Aaron's parental leave. It has been a disturbing, and slightly dystopian process in which our family exists yet is not recognized on paper. This kind of thing has happened to other families in years since. He took extra time off work to take care of me, which we couldn't prove happened because we were too busy in the middle of it all. Things would have been a little faster if we'd enlisted as a cis family. We didn't want our support payments to be delayed or withdrawn due to a mismatch in gender markers on our welfare support application, which had happened to us before and I've heard, sadly, since as well. The system is being reformed by a lot of thoughtful people, but it is still a system designed within structures of oppression. So we never got the full financial support yet somehow made it through several months, overdrawing on past socioeconomic smarts. I'm a little fearful to say more. We do receive some social security payment but have stopped trying to file for the full amount that we would qualify for. We had to leave the in-person appointment to record that we were adding another child to our household because the lighting and ambient noise were giving me a migraine. The local area manager came out with us, apologized, and saw us on our way, with me gagging and stumbling in Aaron's arms. It is the system that causes harm not the folks who work in these spaces, as bewildering and belittling as it felt.

A few days after this encounter, news flowed through to us about the death of a friend. The friend left a note. In it, the friend asked that we not pass blame—that they were trying to survive and are now, instead, part of a matter cycle that we can all stop and take notice of, together. Loved and chosen family, dear ones and queer ones held memorials around the country both off and online, which we attend with both our children held close. But on the morning we first heard, I silently wobbled myself outside and down the street, approaching a familiar fruit tree. Its leaves gave us a yellow carpet on which to take a family-and-belly-bump picture in the autumn. Now, there were leaf buds, almost at swell point, like me. There were thorns covering the branches, telling creatures who may stop by "not yet but soon." I smiled at this tree, feeling prickly and swollen, too. I traced the bark and thought it looked like stretch mark scars.

Later, our doula straddled the space seamlessly between playing with our older child and bodyguarding. Aaron and I, along with our midwife, ran an internal swab stick in our bed to determine if I'd shed some amniotic fluid or leukorrhea, the former of which means a hospital transfer. Not the end of it all, and certainly physically safer, but still not something I wanted. Test cleared, but by the LMP count, we were forty-one weeks. I felt external and internal pressure to begin birthing before we aged out of the homebirth program and all the peace, privacy, ally building, and friendships formed along this gestation. All parties agreed birthing was close enough to prepare the special pool in our living room, next to the medical kit and oxygen tanks delivered just in case. Some beloved friends took care of our child at their home for the weekend. I finally cried about the recent political history, cried for our dead friend, hydrated, and then cried some more for my pelvic pain that seemed to stay no matter whether or how I moved. I cried for the earth and the problems I wasn't actively fighting because I was busy existing. Aaron cried, too. We held each other until I needed to sit down.

Another week passed and our older child was happily back with us. We queued up calming soundscape clips and ridiculous comedies after their bedtime. After some pain relief, gentle stretches, and cuddles, I had a break from my brain fog. It was fleeting, but this allowed me to miss a few close friends and family. I had not been far from my bedroom in a month, unable to reach out to them as they went through respective major life events as well. I dozed and dreamed of the perfect home birth in calm water. This happened again the next night with the dream version of our baby telling me two different names. I saw galaxies reflected in their newborn gaze. All the crying and laughing and waiting and dozing in and out for days built up. I laughed at a pretty throw-away line on the show me and Aaron were curled up watching, after an afternoon spent on a family walk to shake off cabin fever. The cat gave us both a slow blink of respect before being confined to a separate room. I rolled over, thinking I needed the loo, moving slowly so as not to wake the child across the hallway and instead soaked the bed with fresh, salty, clear, and healthy amniotic fluid. What a shock and a relief. I wobbled to the edge of the bed at one minute to eleven in the evening. We joked about narrowly making deadline before the routine labour induction. Aaron helped put my soothing playlist on from just my phone, a placeholder for the better system out near the birthing pool. He closed the child's bedroom door, so I was freer to vocalize my pain, and made me heat packs while informing the midwives and doula to fly into action. I became everywhere and nowhere all at once.

I felt my soft bed in front and sturdy floor beneath. I smelled rain. I closed my eyes and saw eyelid etchings like dancing lightning that time to my heartbeat. I touched slowly inside myself between surges. *Those lines went the opposite direction yesterday* was my last thought before I counted, breathing, roaring to let the efforts go up rather than bear down too soon, allowing my bendy places time to knit and my knitted places time to bend. Time twisted in all directions around us. The fetal head crowned into my hand, a quick pulse against my own, almost as quick.

Suddenly, I was aware that I was **not** alone. Aaron was just beside the doorway, following the instructions to notify an ambulance as per insurance requirements. I didn't want to go anywhere or see anyone. Wrapping myself in the nightscape of home, I felt like I might fall asleep. I manually opened my eyes to ground myself but the shades of wetness around me, the metal and wet fabric scents, overrode and I believed I might not awaken. I launched towards verbal language again. I wanted to communicate it all, to say "I love you," but I got stuck in the first vowel.

Time must have passed with me holding the being between my legs, between worlds. The doula padded softly to my side. *It sounds like she has fuzzy socks on and WHY am I getting this information to my brain when I'm birthing right now?!*

"Saige. You are birthing your baby beautifully right now." She talked us through, just enough for comfort, never superfluous. I was doing a good enough job all along. I really just needed to hear it from someone else. At midnight, we geeked and gawked for a moment at our placenta construction as I caught it in a plastic bag above the bathroom drain. The doula led me to the bed. Our midwife carried the attached placenta, and Aaron carried the newborn. Someone had turned off the background sounds and layered clean blankets.

It started to rain hard. I breathed, hard.

A smile flitted among us. The protocol ambulance arrived outside. The baby kicked. I snipped the cord to create the final touch, an adorable outie bellybutton.

A few strange hours in the hospital otherworld, transfusions and repair for me while nestling my newborn the entire time, protected by our midwife and her taped-on sign in texta

Thank you for respecting this family's privacy. Please see file at front desk and knock before entering.

And we were home. into a wilderness of cuddles, sleeplessness, love, and hormone rollercoasters. The Raynaud's symptoms were harder to manage. My chest became engorged; it felt like it was something foreign and stuck on. I was irritable to the rest of my family and uncomfortable when I wasn't in outright pain. The baby's latch and patience were wonderful; the peaceful snuggles of the early days I will always hold in my heart. We reached out to our team and friends again and I was supported to suppress lactation and use formula, even though ten generous families and more networks of friends who drive got amazing human milk donations to our doorstep. I do still feel mournful about this, even though we made the best choices possible to us in that time.

Before I knew it, three whole months of human milk and prosthetic chestfeeding via bottle had taken place. Our baby was utterly thriving by the time their paperwork came in the mail, correctly marked this time with a father, a parent, a sibling, and an unspecified gender marker, as a placeholder to allow self-expression (Myers). Before I knew it, it was the following spring, and I wiggled my way off the lumpy double bed, wondering when the next time would be that I'd cuddle the two children to sleep like that. It was the night before my top surgery, and again, I was thinking I might not make it through alive. *Better be alright, Saige,* I thought. *My crowd-funders need me to thank them properly.*

Aaron held me around the waist. I cupped my chest in thanks for its coziness and nourishment of infants, ready to uncover my authentic shape. We both wondered aloud what hugs might be like post operatively.

"See you on the other side, Love." I got him to smirk with that, although parting at a hospital again was hard.

When all the interviews, monitors, and protocols had me prepped for theatre, I replayed the feeling of his eyes twinkling with that silent laugh as I went under. Terrified, I tried to speak up to the operating staff. I have no idea what came out, but in my head, it was clear: *I'm trans-forming my chest. I can't thank you enough for your help.* I didn't know if my heart rate would be safe enough, but it turns out all of me was kept safe by staff who followed medical policy documents and adapted to my senses and abilities without batting an eyelid.

Before it felt like I could catch my breath, probably the binding compression vest they have you wear, my family of four were out on the beach, touching slimy seaweed and counting coal freighters on the horizon.

A cousin, professionally a midwife, took me for a life-affirming coffee at a local café when I was cleared for short walks. This kindness was parallel to a call from my homebirth team's admin stating that deidentified stats and conclusions about "all the women" from the program was about to go to press. A surgical drain slipped from my carry bag, leaking. Discerning Cousin saw this and immediately plugged it back in before a single air bubble could form. Fumbling my napkins onto fresh stains, we laughed that I'd spilled transition fluid at a swanky east-side cafe. I put away my phone and permitted myself a single sigh so as not to jostle my grafts and stitching.

Part Five: Recovery Transformed

The fire season lasted through another early spring as I wrote to you. I wore my compression vest. My children relearned to climb me as I tried not to lift them, waiting, and rebuilding my strength in my new form with strict exercise and rest.

Each morning before the family brekky rush, I pick up my Velcro braces from the seat where our old cat cocoons himself these days and wrap the right places with just enough pressure to match my inner strength to the corporeal. Once everyone's ready, I affirm with my daily testosterone dose in the last quiet moment in this home.

Outside, the latest generation of magpie fledglings hop and hunt with their parents. Aaron usually carries our canes; then Daddy and Papa Zazza link hands with Rueben who will squeeze our palms in rhythm, sharing the sounds she hears.

Meanwhile, Aster who is self-declared to be "not a baby, just me and my words." sometimes asks what pronouns the birds use ("Words birds love? We don't know yet, so we say "'they'.") Or dangles a stretchy shoestring end from hand to hand, singing in a stage whisper ("That's alright, I'm three now so I don't run away, I run *with* you and take this sparkley-um. This you-see-me thingy!") To which Rueben quickly relates the specifics of where and when we got the shoelace.

The daylight burns, but it is also dazzling, welcoming as we adventure as far as weather, disaster recovery, walking a cat on a leash, Lockdowns and respecting immune systems permit. Warmth melts my pain away for long enough that I can notice the cold breeze tugging my mask on the way to the local walking trails.

I leave you with a promise of hope, since, Reader, our collective future is ever more uncertain. With whatever happens next, we can all show up for one another and find pride in our authentic selves, whether quietly in our chrysalises, donning a facemask at a protest, raising a wave in solidarity from bedrest, raising children—all of this, or some other. Our acts of fierceness and kinder change are always a necessary metamorphosis.

Works Cited

Faa, Marian. "Indigenous Leaders Say Australia's Bushfire Crisis Shows Approach to Land Management Failing." *Australian Broadcast*

Corporation, 13 Nov. 2019, www.abc.net.au/news/2019-11-14/traditional-owners-predicted-bushfire-disaster/11700320. Accessed 21 Oct. 2021.

McKenzie, Sheena. "How Australia's 'Everyday Racism' Moved from Political Fringe to Mainstream Media." *CNN* 16 April 2019, edition. cnn.com/2019/04/15/australia/australia-racism-media-christchurch-attack-intl/index.html. Accessed 21 Oct. 2021.

Myers, Kyl. *Raising Zoomer*, 2021, www.raisingzoomer.com/. Accessed 21 Oct. 2021.

Purkis, Yenn, et al. *The Autistic Trans Guide to Life.* Jessica Kingsley Publishers, 2021.

Chapter 8

Towards a Queer and Trans Model for Families of Colour: Intersections of Feminism, Race, Queerness, and Gender Identity

Jan E. Estrellado and Alanna Aiko Moore

Introduction

When we decided to become parents, we knew we would be trying to fit ourselves as parents and our new family into a society and institutional systems that are not designed for us and do not include us. We knew queer family-making would be truly intersectional in our understanding of where our parenting intersects with race, class, gender, and sexuality. Seven years later, we are navigating this new terrain. Alanna is a mixed-race Asian queer femme (she/her/hers) married to Jan, a Pilipinx, queer, transmasculine, and non-binary person (who responds to all pronouns). We have two amazing children: "K." age seven (who currently identifies as a boy), and "A." age five (who currently identifies as a girl). From prepregnancy on, we have fought heteronormative stereotypes about gender and what parents should look like; reminded countless medical providers that all forms should be parent one/parent two rather than mother/father; explained to daycare providers that our children have a "mama" and "dada" (even if they see two moms); and interrupted racism in the educational curriculum. Parenting with our intersectional identities is a constant struggle against systematic oppression, which ties family values and family belonging solely to white, cisgender, heterosexual, and middleclass folks. Queer and trans parenting while brown can be a precarious existence, and a lack of stability can be found in many areas of our lives. Finally, in this legal and social climate, how do we parent without fear? Hate crimes against folks who are brown, queer, and especially trans* are on the rise. How do we tell our children there are people who hate us because of how we look and who we love, that businesses can choose not to serve us, and that policies threaten our civil rights and strip us of our humanity? How do we continue to be subversive (since parenting with our identities leave us no other choice) while keeping everyone safe? And finally, how do we capture joy, hope, and possibility and pass them on to our children as well?

In this chapter, we attempt to offer prospects about family structure and parenting practices based on our values. The term "model," as noted in the chapter's title, is based less on specific parameters or rules and more on the possibilities that racial justice, gender creativity, and feminist values can present in parenting.

Language and Naming (Jan)

Traditional structures of language and naming within parenting and family models reinforce not only heteropatriachy but also whiteness, monogamy, and capitalism (Few-Demo et al. 75; Penelope 390). Contradictions occur when examining our particular family structure. When our oldest child was born six years ago, not only did we ask ourselves what we wished to be called but also what it meant (emotionally, socially, and politically) to be called by that name. Alanna chose "Mama," and I did not choose anything, deferring to the children to choose a name that fit how they think of me. The result was that the older child chose "Dada" and the younger one followed suit.

The consequence of my choice (not to choose) is that for the first few years of K's life, he thought that his family was just like other families (i.e., one mom and one dad). In an attempt to be queer allies and teach other children to be accepting of difference, some of his preschool teachers and other parents would talk about how K. had two moms.

When his understanding conflicted with others' perceptions of a homonormative parenting structure (i.e., two moms), he had strong negative reactions to people's lack of understanding about our family. Around the age of four, K. would angrily insist that he had "one mama and one dada." He could clearly see that his family was not mirrored in others' perceptions of our family. This initially puzzled his well-meaning (and otherwise amazing) teachers as well as some of the parents of the other children who were taken aback, uncomfortable, and unfamiliar with the correct language to use. Other parents would ask Alanna but not me directly about my gender identity, perhaps for fear of offending me. The parenting dilemma here was how we would respond to others' misperceptions of my gender identity. Should I express outrage, correct the misperception, appear nonplussed, or ignore it? Ultimately, context tends to be one of the most critical factors. If I have an investment in the relationship with the misperceiver, I might gently correct ("K refers to me as Dada."). If I have no investment in the relationship and/or do not plan on seeing this person after this interaction, I usually ignore it. I have reassured both children that it does not bother me (which is largely true) and to explain why people think of me this way. What usually follows after I reassure them is a string of doubts about whether my choice was the right choice, anger that I even had to make a choice, and then some level of acceptance in order to move on to the next thing in my day. Much of the invisible labour related to this education tends to fall on Alanna as a trans ally. It can be awkward for Alanna to manage other people's scrutiny of me and our family: their assumptions, rabid interest, and objectification of my body. Alanna struggles with how to explain (often in passing hallway conversations) gender neutral pronouns as well as how to define trans and gender non-binary while also managing her annoyance and anger at being asked to do this invisible labour. At times, she chooses not to engage or come out because it is exhausting, time-consuming, and offers nothing in return. Alanna has often remarked that explaining "two moms" would be easier, since there is a larger mainstream acceptance and knowledge of that model, more resources, and representation; but our beautiful family is more complex and gender-expansive than mainstream models typically offer.

Both children have a fairly nuanced understanding of gender for their age. K. and A. comprehend that people understand their gender as more than and sometimes differently than their body parts. They also acknowledge that there are more than two ways to identify a person's gender. When asked how they describe my gender, K. or A. might say something like, "You're part girl and part boy, but you have a girl's body," or "You have a girl body and a boy brain" (a nod to the 2014 book *I Am Jazz* by transgender youth activist Jazz Jennings). Our kids have not only accepted the expansiveness of gender but seem to embrace and celebrate it, both in themselves and in others. It is truly one of the parenting accomplishments of which I am most proud. I have often had the thought, as I know many queer, trans, and ally parents do, that if it is so simple for our children to understand these concepts, why is it so difficult for so many adults to do the same?

One area where I can see the acceptance of my gender identity is bathroom selection and use. K. will often want to go to the bathroom with me and tends to prefer using urinals. I've often had the conversation with him that sometimes I feel unsafe entering either bathroom, depending on what I wear, where I am, and who is around. Now, he will usually ask me which bathroom I feel most comfortable in before choosing one. Recently, after entering the men's restroom, he shared, "Don't worry, Dada. I'll make sure you're safe in here." While my heart swelled with love and pride, I also experienced some degree of sadness that my son already knows that the bathroom—where we address our basic needs and also can feel exceptionally vulnerable—can potentially be an unsafe place for his parent.

One of my fears about being a genderqueer, transmasculine parent is that my children would be embarrassed or burdened by my gender identity. I am cautiously anticipating this experience as both kids enter elementary school and peer influence becomes stronger. How will they talk about me with their friends? Will they become ashamed that my gender identity confuses people? And when they arrive at the ages when they'll do anything to avoid standing out from the crowd, will they be embarrassed to say that I am their parent? Although I can fully take responsibility for these being my fears and not Alanna's or our children's fears, I also acknowledge that these fears did not come from me alone. Messages about being undesirable, less than, and an abomination have been present in implicit and explicit ways over the course of my lifetime, not only by societal standards and systems of power but also interpersonally by acquaintances, friends, and family members. While I have worked relentlessly not to live my life from those messages, I cannot deny their presence or their influence on my fears about what kind of parent my children got but did not choose.

When we started connecting with other queer families, I was surprised that many of the other queer parents we met tended to stick to gender binary names for themselves with their children. I was certain that there would be more non-binary, trans, masculine-identified parents who would use gender non-binary or nonconforming names, and of course, a few have (Fairyington). I have asked myself why trans, especially non-binary and gender-creative parents, might use gender binary names. Am I making assumptions about a person's gender identity based on the name they use? I remind myself to own my judgmental thoughts and to respect the rights of parents everywhere to name themselves. The other, more important (and less judgmental) question is do we (queer and trans parents) choose normative names because we lack models for naming possibilities that more accurately reflect gender diversity? I tend to lean in this direction because the more queer and trans parents I meet, the more I am starting to see the range of name possibilities. "MaPa," "MaDa," "Mady," and "Zaza" are just a few of the non-binary options available to today's queer and trans parents (Mombian). Our young queer and trans people will of course continue to push our communities to the forefront on gender expansiveness, and as this generation will at some point begin their own families, I suspect there will be an explosion of new parenting names available in our lexicon.

Invisible Labour (Jan)

The Burden of Multiple Oppressions

Both of us knew when we started a family that we were bound to continue encountering different kinds of oppression. We are a queer and trans multiracial family. What we did not anticipate is how our experiences of oppression would shift after having kids.

As many families of colour do, we anticipated how we wanted to socialize our children around issues of race and ethnicity. We were particularly focused on making sure our kids grew up around people of colour and that models for antiracism practice were deeply integrated into their upbringing. Instilling pride in their racial and ethnic identities continues to be a priority, especially given that they have multiple ethnic heritages. We curate their book collection to make sure that their texts feature kids of colour, selectively choose which television shows and movies highlight positive, realistic portrayals of people of colour, and attend community events, including protests and rallies, that highlight the importance of people of colour in our lives and reflect their realities as young kids of colour.

The gender socialization of our children is a parallel process to their education around race and ethnicity. We want our kids to have flexibility around their gendered choices while also informing them of the possible responses they might get from others. We talk about the power of language (using "everybody" instead of "guys") and provide a wide range of choices around toys, clothes, colours, and interests. As they enter the K-12 school system, we proactively discuss our views about gender with their teachers to see how collaboratively we can continue that education during the week.

As I reflect on the gender and racial socialization of our children, I am struck by how much time, energy, money, and labour we spend that some other families do not. What have other families chosen to do with the time that they likely did not know they had? How many more zoo or park trips might they have taken while we were preparing presentations, picking books, having conversations with teachers, or having conversations with each other about how to approach a particular race- or gender-focused topic? In our professional lives, each of us gets paid to provide trainings and presentations on social justice topics, including antiracism, antisexism, as well as queer- and trans-affirming practices. In the realm of parenting, however, this has not only been largely uncompensated, but also largely invisible and unseen to most people. Not until the time of this writing have I reflected on the level of internal and external resources expended on these efforts to provide a safe and affirming environment for our children.

Consequences of Invisible Labour

One consequence of engaging in this type of invisible labour is the toll on emotional health, but due to its invisible nature, it is expected and mostly obligational. As soon as the question is asked ("Would you and Alanna be willing to provide a training on..."), in the service of our children's wellbeing, we often say "yes." The burden of living at the intersections of multiple oppressions is that we do, in fact, want these questions to be asked and answered. We both want that education to be taught, and we want to preserve our own time and energy for ourselves, each other, and our kids.

Most of the consequences I have experienced are related to my own health. For many years, I struggled to take good care of my physical health. Anger was a familiar response to systemic and interpersonal oppression as a young queer Filipinx person of colour. That anger was turned outwards to some degree (I was not particularly pleasant to be around for a few years in college), but it also turned inwards. I smoked however many cigarettes I wanted, usually after having eaten whatever I'd wanted. I'd had a years-long case of the "fuck-its." Having had now decades of personal growth since that time, I can acknowledge that these feelings were not only anger but also deeply internalized shame about my perceived unattractiveness and rage about how unfair it was that I was not valued the way many cisgender, heterosexual (hereafter referred to as "cis-het") people were. It took me many years to treat my body with the respect and honour it deserves, and now in my forties, I consider caring for my physical health to be part of my social justice practice. Mostly due to habit, however, my physical health continues to be an area of my life that I often neglect first when the stress of living in my world becomes too great.

I wonder how other queer and trans parents of colour cope. I admit that I feel hopeful at the thought that my coping responses may not be unique to me. I informally asked the queer and trans parents of colour I know on social media about the costs of invisible labour for their lives. Feelings of anger, resentment, rejection, and disappointment were common emotional responses to the space that invisible labour occupies in their lives. For some, invisible labour used up limited internal resources, often in addition to other stressors that already affected parenting (e.g., being working class, single parenting, being a multi-racial family, and living in a geographical area with little to no queer folks and/or people of colour). The emotional intensity of our community's responses was palpable. It was clear that so many of us engaged in invisible labour, often with the feeling that we had to do it because it was for our kids and that this deeply affected us.

I consider us fortunate to have a significant number of queer people of colour with children in our lives, both personally and professionally.

The shared camaraderie and friendship with our community is a lifeline for both of us. It is certainly one positive outcome from the pain of invisible labour—that we get to share our struggles and triumphs with likeminded others. There is beauty in not needing to explain why parenting is exhausting in the multiple ways it is. We are not just raising our kids (which any parent knows is already exhausting). We are also trying to change the world around us so that our kids can move about the world more freely than perhaps we had the opportunity to do.

Lack of Visible, Diverse Family Models

Despite the great fortune of being around other queer and trans families of colour, it is still true that we have limited access to a diversity of family models. It is hard to describe to those who do not share our intersectional identities the cumulative feeling that we are often the only queer or trans family of colour we will see on a daily basis. Feelings of resentment bubble up as I think about the ease that other families who align with whiteness and cis-het normativity have in the world, especially because most lack insight of the privileges this affords them as a family.

The counterpoint to this, of course, is that on the rare occasion that we do get to see another queer or trans family of colour, we have often become fast friends. The look of relief and acknowledgment in a brief moment of eye contact is evident. Given our children's ages, I'm quite certain this level of support is more for us as parents than for our children, but I hope that someday our children can appreciate how hard we have worked to shape an environment for them where they can see themselves in those around them.

Parenting Practices (Alanna)

Queer and trans models of parenting mean we make choices every day that run counter to heteronormative family structures and that we actively work to reshape the core concepts of what a family is and what it looks like. Being parents of colour means we also make different choices on the daily on how to raise our children. We make choices on how to parent in a world that is dominated by homophobia, transphobia, white privilege, and white supremacy. Living while queer, trans and as people of colour also means that we parent in precarity and face insufficient systems of support. We continue to persevere as parents of colour and refuse to have our family erased in a white, heteronormative world.

We knew getting pregnant was going to be intentional, with no chance of getting "knocked up" like heterosexual folks and were clear that we wanted to parent in an intersectional way. This led us to schedule several "retreats" (really, three hour coffee dates) where we discussed what we wanted our intersectional queer parenting to look like. During these retreats, we talked about what our parenting philosophies were, what social conventions we wanted to reject, and things we did not want to replicate from our own experiences of being parented. We agreed that I would be the gestational parent and that we wanted equity in parenting from the beginning. Jan attended as many of my appointments as possible, and we tried to minimize the pregnancy's effects on each other's careers. We did not want to reproduce behaviours we experienced as children from our parents such as a lack of communication, emotional neglect, explosive anger and physical punishment. We also acknowledged that we would be creating our own path, with few parenting models that reflected our identities and experiences.

One parenting priority on which we agreed was honesty with our children. We keep it real. We were honest with the kids from the age of three that they were conceived via sperm donor and shared, in general, how the process took place. We talk about the hard stuff: power, privilege, and oppression. We emphasize the value of Black and brown people and queer and trans lives and pride in our culture and ancestry. We teach our children in age-appropriate ways about racism, homophobia, sexism, xenophobia, ableism, classism, and other forms of oppression. We discuss how gender is fluid and how they should ask people they meet for pronouns. Being honest in this way means parenting as activists and expecting our children to be activists, too. We want our children to interrupt oppression when they witness it, to stand up for others, and to be a strong ally to others. We want them to be changemakers. We want them to know that they can love who they want. That being said, we also feel a sense of responsibility for future hardships they may experience because of who their parents are, how we identify, and how we present our gender identities.

Selecting the Best Fit School For Our Children

We were privileged in having some choice in where our children attended elementary school. Beyond the neighborhood school one is zoned for, there was also a district ability to choose from a variety of schools based on a lottery system. Having access to more options caused us to ask many questions as we tried to find a school that met all of our ideals. We asked ourselves the following:

- Will our queer family of colour with a trans/non-binary parent be accepted?
- Will grown-ups mirror our family so that our children feel validated and seen?
- How might our children respond if they feel unseen, and how would we support them through that?
- How much education might we have to provide for others, usually for free?
- How much time will that emotional labour draw away from other important social justice work we do professionally and personally?

We both wished to be with other queer and trans families but also to be around other people of colour. We toured many schools where we would have been "the only"—the only queer family, the only trans parent, or one of the only brown families in the whole school.

Then we found what seemed like a unicorn: a school with a social justice focus and that supported Jan's gender identity, our queerness, and our children's gender nonconforming choices (K. likes to wear dresses on occasion). There were queer and trans staff and parents at the school. Several classmates were gender nonconforming. Discussions of pronouns, including they/them, were part of the curriculum. The children acknowledged different skin colours and talked about what that meant. We felt seen, accepted, and part of a community.

One year later, due to administrative negligence at the highest leadership levels, the school we loved began to disintegrate. We transferred K. to our neighborhood school, seven weeks into the start of the school year.

We worried whether teachers and administration at the new school would understand our family. Much time was taken to craft supportive, positive, and collaborative emails that also communicated our wish to be seen and acknowledged as a multiracial, queer, and trans family. As people of colour, we are always burdened with being both palatable to mostly white, cisgender, and heterosexual parents while also fiercely advocating for our family. This emotional labour amplified the expected stress of transitioning to a new school environment.

In K.'s new school, cisnormativity and heteronormativity are deeply embedded. For example, while helping with homework, we encountered the following prompt: "Dad has a red _____." The choices included "nest," "tent," "desk," and "truck." The correct answer was truck. K. and Jan discussed this at length: Couldn't Mom have a red truck? What about Dad having a red nest? Most parent examples in the classroom curriculum reference two parents: a mom and a dad. No other family models are discussed. Most of the people in the books and exercises are white. Language and reading are powerful forces shaping our children's minds and yet, at age six, K. is already exposed to a world that does not reflect his own. We understand that the system of education was created and maintained by white, cis-het people and was never meant for families like ours. Although the work required to challenge gender stereotypes and cis-het normativity feels inconvenient on the best days and unrelenting on the worst, we also feel a deep commitment to create representation and space for all underrepresented families, who have too often been invisible.

Being one of the few queer families in K.'s school, I often internalize and worry about judgment from other parents, staff, and teachers. When K. has experienced challenges transitioning to his new school, I wondered if people had thoughts that were not just about his actual behavior issues: "Yes, that's the LGBT family with the problem kid." "He must be having a hard time because his parents are gay and parent differently." "Well, the family life is sinful, maybe not stable, so it makes sense that he is having issues." To be honest, I have no idea if parents and staff are thinking these transphobic and homophobic thoughts, but because of our identities, we know that cis-het, white folks make judgments based on our identities. Because of our identities we, as parents, will often have to wonder or work harder towards "normalcy" in order to be accepted.

Social Consequences

These fears about judgment bleed into other areas of our parenting lives, too. K. recently chose new sneakers. They were shiny silver sneakers with pink glitter trim and purple accents. These are the shoes he wanted, yet I hesitated before adding them to my online cart. My first thought: I didn't want him to have another hurdle, since there was a possibility that he would be teased that the shoes were too girly. I know cis-het parents also have these worries when a child bucks male stereotypes, but the pressure and scrutiny are more intense as a queer family.

Other social consequences of our parenting identities include lack of support and community. There are dozens of mom groups both in my area and online, but they are overwhelmingly cis-het and white. I have ventured into these spaces when I was desperate for support, also fully cognizant that I would have to engage in a conversation about how they were defining "mom" and whether Jan would be welcome as a trans parent. It soon became apparent that the group defined "mom" as "not-dad," or not a straight, cisgender man.

Conclusion

The burden on queer and trans families of colour is great. The pressure to raise our children with our values, coupled with shaping an environment that is not made for our family, can be daunting and exhausting. We aim to nurture pride in our children based on who they are, where they come from, and where their people come from. We hope that our choices to change the world around them in small, meaningful ways engender their own activism and commitment to social justice. Our family, who are in many ways just trying to exist the way most families do, offers one example of the added complexities related to feminism, race, queerness, and transness.

Works Cited

Fairyington, Stephanie. "Some L.G.B.T. Parents Reject the Names 'Mommy' and 'Daddy.'" *New York Times*, 26 Apr. 2018, www.nytimes.com/2018/04/26/well/family/some-lgbt-parents-reject-the-names-mommy-and-daddy.html. Accessed 21 Oct. 2021.

Few-Demo, April L., et al. "Queer Theory, Intersectionality, and LGBT Parent Families: Transformative Critical Pedagogy in Family Theory." *Journal of Family Theory & Review,* vol. 8, no. 1, 2016, pp. 74-94.

Mombian. "A Parent by Any Other Name: What Our Kids Call Us, Redux." *Mombian,* 26 Apr. 2018, www.mombian.com/2018/04/26/ a-parent-by-any-other-name-what-our-kids-call-us-redux/ ?fbclid =IwAR2CJC_ihNXTVUJ_BYhMP4hkn38DKfRkArMxlPK7JllT 70q0Ndns2lPxD-4. Accessed 21 Oct. 2021.

Penelope, Julia. "Language and the Transformation of Consciousness." *Law & Inequality: A Journal of Theory and Practice,* vol. 4, no. 2, 1986, pp. 379-391.

Chapter 9

An Interview with Pidgeon

Kori Doty

K: Can you tell us a little bit about yourself and how you became involved with the activism and advocacy work that you do?

P: My name is Pidgeon Pagonis. I was born intersex but did not know I was intersex until I was eighteen. And when I found out I was shocked. I wanted to figure out a way, eventually, after I got rid of some of the shame and fear ... to come out publicly and talk about my story and also figure out a way to stop what happened to me from happening to other people in the future. I was eighteen. I was in college, and I worked intersex research into my thesis at school. I got to meet activists that way, from the first waves of intersex activism, which was awesome. It really set the stage for me to see that—to not just *read* about intersex activism but meet the people that started it and be inspired by them to take that legacy on and to add to it. So, that's how it started.

K: That's really cool that you got a chance to have in-person relationships with the lineage.

P: Yes. Still do. We're a pretty small community, a tight-knit community of people.

K: This collection is about moving beyond the binary in reproduction and parenting. We're working to identify and deconstruct binaries that relate to sex, gender, sexuality, parenting roles, and even things like infertility, fertility, wanted or unwanted pregnancies, unfit or fit parents, etc. Do you think that it's important to move beyond the binary when it comes to how we think and talk about reproduction and parenting life? If so, why?

P: Duh, yeah! Everything! ... I don't think anything should be talked about in a binary framework, ever. Yeah, I really hate the binary, in all shapes and forms. So, of course, ... I would hate it when talking about reproduction, babies, families, and all of that. So, yeah, and then, the why—I know in my DNA, in my soul, in my body, in my heart, in my mind that nothing exists in an either/or category 100 per cent. Nothing. Humans, plants, pets, or anything on this earth, anything in space. Everything. I just think that the desire to trap that diversity of existence into an either/or category makes sense because it makes some things easier. If you are speaking power over something and you want to say, "I have power over you. There are only two categories, and I'm the smartest and the fastest, and that's why I have power over you." So, I see why people do that, but it just limits the way we understand each other and the world and not always in positive ways. And it ends up with gender and sex, as you can see from examples of countless intersex people who are born just existing, and born with a body that I define as being outside of the binary, you see this: When binary frameworks are applied to conceptualizing our bodies and our genders, you see the harm that follows. And I think that is completely rooted in binary thinking about sex and gender. When it comes to reproduction, I just feel like there is an extension of that harm. So, for instance, when I was a kid, my mom had to break the news to me, as the doctors had instructed her to, to tell me I couldn't have kids. So, basically that I was infertile. And she said, "Don't worry. You can adopt a baby." But I think that binary way of thinking was then passed onto me. I guess because the powers that be—my doctors, my surgeons, people in society, my mom, my dad—couldn't conceptualize reproduction or family making outside of a heteronormative framework and binary. They see it as this really sad thing, that they had to tell me. Like, "Oh, you can't have children biologically, so you can do this, adopt." And like those are the only two options in the world. And also, it was seen as like it had to be done in a heterosexual way, too. I think what it ends up doing is limiting possibility and imagination. I think we're all born with these beautiful imaginations, and I think that the binary lenses that we are forced to wear as we grow up do great damage to our ability to imagine multiplicity in all things. And, so, the same happens with reproduction. Defining someone as just fertile or infertile, it's so interesting. That doesn't even make sense really because I feel like people are various shades of fertile and different times of the month and different chances. Like, if you don't carry a baby to term, are you infertile? Or are you fertile? In a binary world, you are either one of those things, and people would probably say that you're infertile. But I think that's a perfect example of a grey zone or a multiplicity, a way of understanding fertility, because this person was fertile, could conceive a child or a fetus, and make that fetus happen for a while. So, I think it casts people into these simplified boxes that I don't think people were ever meant to be in. I don't think it helps anybody, these either/or boxes.

K: Yeah, and that back and forth about infertility like you were saying in that example. It's interesting because for me, in my experience, when I had my first miscarriage, the doctors responded and said, "Well, the good thing that we know, at least, is that you are fertile." Because I was capable of conceiving.

P: Oh, interesting. So, maybe I was wrong, and they do consider that fertile.

K: But I feel like if you had a number of miscarriages, a number of pregnancies that didn't result in a live birth, then you would be considered infertile. So, there is this grey area, and I think this is the whole thing about humans, our diversity and complexity. When you try to put us into boxes, there will always be outliers, and a part of our function in the world as outliers is to demonstrate that the boxes are made up.

P: Yeah. And were you trans, you said?

K: Yeah. And I had taken some hormones before trying to conceive, so there was some question.... My doctors at the time were like—and this was almost ten years ago—"We don't know the impacts of testosterone on fertility." And I was like, "Well, I do, because I know a bunch of other guys who have gotten pregnant after being on testosterone. So, I know, because anecdotally and within our community, but the medical research—you think you don't know!"

P: That's interesting. I would have hypothesized that or guessed that because you were taking hormones. I think that might shift the way that they view your fertility. It would be seen as like, "Well, thankfully you're still fertile. You didn't ruin that part of your womanhood, or whatever the fuck they think." But I think if it was a woman, a cis woman, they might see that person as like a broken woman and not fertile.

K: Totally.

P: And that's just a hunch I have. That the circumstances and who they are speaking to affect how they describe fertility. Also, at the same time, they might say, "You're super fertile, but you can't take it to term."

K: There's the things that the doctors say, and then all the things that we say to ourselves because we've internalized them. The doctors don't even need to say them, right; we tell them to ourselves.

P: I think also we get more microscopic. If we think about hormones in the binary world— women have estrogen and men have testosterone. And that's a great myth. Most people have both and more flowing through their bodies. We grew up with this myth, you know, that women have estrogen and men have testosterone. Not you and I—we know different now. But I grew up with that myth, and the truth is it's not that binary. It's not a binary at all. Everybody has different amounts. I think the same thing. When you realize that that's not true, then you can chip away at the false binary myth that only cis women can be fertile. I have a feeling there are some haters out there who are like maybe if there was a cis man who could take estrogen and have a uterus implant one day and ovary implant, I bet there would be haters out there who would be like, "Oh, you're not fertile. You're fake fertile." But it's like, "No! It's all part of a spectrum. There is no infertile and fertile, there's just different ranges of it." And, like, is a woman who goes through menopause and maybe she had ten kids, is she no longer considered fertile? I don't know. It depends on a lot of factors and who is asking. And does having ten kids make you more fertile than the person who has one? You don't know! And then that comes into play with intersex people so much. They claim to try to always preserve fertility when they are making decisions about intersex kids' bodies, without their consent, but they rarely ever do. And because they see fertility in a binary sense—and they don't understand looking at it from a queer framework or a trans framework or anything else besides the binary, hetero framework—they will do things like castrate intersex kids all the time because they see their testes, their undescended testes as not being in line with the gender that they're going to assign that kid, surgically and hormonally. So, for me, I was assigned female, and I had undescended testes and they were like, "Oh, let's throw those away." They claim that they care about fertility, but if the kid doesn't fit into their binary understanding of sex and gender, they can't even see the fertility potential in that person. So my main point is that conceiving of reproduction through or via a binary lens limits or obscures fertility potential in intersex people. For intersex people, I can't tell you how many of us have gotten our undescended testes surgically removed because the doctors decided that we were going to be women and that we had no use for testes. But they don't know. In the future, there could be a procedure invented or created that could harvest sperm or some type of living material like DNA from our testes that allows us to have sperm, which would allow us to be fertile. But because they can only see us in a binary lens and thus pathologize us because we don't fit within that binary lens. Our bodies mess up the whole basis that they are operating from when it comes to their definitions of infertility and fertility. It reminds me of this quote from *Middlesex*. Cal who is the main narrator says, "If normal was so normal, they could just leave it alone, and let it manifest itself," and so it's the same, I think, with this concept of fertility. If fertility and infertility were normal, and it was only a binary, then they could just leave it alone. But they are always trying to actively construct it in people, and the intersex kind of shines a magnifying glass on what happens to everybody.

K: I really like that. I like the way that that quote is relevant to the topic of fertility because if it was a fixed binary, nobody would access fertility support. Because if you're fertile, you're fertile. You don't have to go to a doctor, take extra hormones, go through IVF. You don't have to increase your fertility because you either are or you aren't. But the reality is that we actually understand that it's flexible, a gradient, and that there are things that we can do that change our relationship to it.

P: As long as it's within the confines of heterosexual relationships, right? Within our culture, at least.

K: That's a good segue into the next question, which is about nonconsensual genital surgery. So we are interested in how these surgeries are done in service of creating and reinforcing the idea of sex as a binary and where these surgeries are an example of reproductive injustice.

P: In terms of reproductive justice, I know that I touched on that by saying that they castrate us depending on the case, but even just removing reproduction, there is an injustice happening in that they are damaging a person's ability to feel sexual satisfaction or pleasure with themselves or with partners and sometimes both. Bo Laurent, who started the Intersex Society of North America (ISNA) said once—either to me, or I read it, or she said it in a documentary, I can't remember. But she talked about how having sex in a pleasurable way is a foundational block of building family. And so, whether you are able to produce babies or not and whether that's because you were born infertile, or you were born fertile or with the potential of fertility—but doctors removed that potential through surgeries that are unnecessary and injustices to intersex people—there is damage done. The damage is done to our flesh, our nerves, our ability to feel sensation. And then there is the trauma that becomes attach to physical interactions that are sexual in nature because of our history of sexual trauma with doctors. How that then becomes attached to things that should be pleasurable with other human beings around our genitalia and our bodies—besides reproductive injustice with intersex kids, there is this other injustice that doesn't get talked about as much—not that reproductive justice gets talked about a lott. Talked about even less is the injustice that comes from making it extremely difficult for a person to become fully integrate into their culture or their community or their society via relationship and family building. It becomes so difficult and traumatic for intersex people who have had their bodily autonomy stripped in really horrific ways to do "normal things," such date and have sex with people, which is more or less a requirement for people to become a couple, stay a couple, stay in a relationship with multiple people, and then to become what we perceive in our culture as a family unit. Especially in a culture like ours in the West, where the dominant narrative is that individualism reigns supreme over community, communal living, and communal family structures, then you are really left out in the cold because you have all these challenges around being able to form ... that nuclear family unit [that] you're supposed to.

Society is structured around that in terms of tax benefits and protections and healthcare, and so you are really doing all of these injustices, on top of taking away a person's reproductive or fertility ability, and [lying] to them about it or [making] sure they weren't full informed about it. There are so many shades of reproductive injustice.

K: Can you speak to some of the activism that has led to policy changes and the ending of nonconsensual and unnecessary surgery on intersex infants in certain places? What brought about those changes and what still needs to happen for those changes to be more common?

P: In the middle of the last century, we see the protocol forming about infancy which has created the current protocol. It was just in its infancy, but that protocol was secrecy, surgery, and shame. With the advent of anesthesia and surgical techniques, people who were once referred to as hermaphrodites and treated a whole host of ways in different times and places or by different cultures were now no longer just passively victims to ostracization or bullying. In the middle of the twentieth century, we see an escalation to removing the parts of that person's body that resulted in their being defined as hermaphrodite in the first place. Now, there is no longer just discursive discrimination, but a very physical thing happening, hormonally and surgically. And then, these kids in the 1950s who were the first batch to have these surgeries done to them grow up. In the 1990s, they find each other for the first time. Part of the protocol was secrecy and shame—to not tell these kids the trust and to tell them that there is no one else like them. It is easier to keep people that you want to control in the dark and isolated from one another. So in the 1990s, Bo Laurent started the Intersex Society of North America as a support group, and she fielded calls from people, created a newsletter, and that became the first wave of intersex activism. Intersex activists have always had to, while doing their activism, create support networks. So that's what came first, creating a soft place for intersex people to meet each other and land, to know each other, to cry with each other. Years later, you see a faction of ISNA doing activism in the streets and in other ways. The first public protest that we know of happened in 1996 on October 26th in Boston, Massachusetts, outside the American Academy of Pediatrics (AAP) conference. You see in the photos and in the articles that people shared on ISNA's website that it was momentus for a generation of people who were told, "There is no one like you" and [were] made to feel freakish, monstrous, and unlovable. Now they were also speaking their truth to the powers that be, the powers of the AAP, and other doctors and surgeons who had harmed them. That was amazing, so we mark that day as Intersex Awareness Day and we just marked our twenty-fourth Intersex Awareness Day. Intersex activism is so multipronged; it's everywhere, in so many different forms, on every continent. It has every method employed, so you have people who work with doctors. You have intersex people who go to medical school and become doctors and try to fix things from the inside. You have people who become lawyers and then fight for intersex human rights using the law and a legal framework. You have human rights activists that are marching and protesting in Europe, the US, and in other countries. You have support groups and conferences happening in South Africa and Uganda. You have legislation being slated in Uganda right now and in Germany, a lot of human rights activism in Australia. And then there is a huge network in Latin America, mostly support and education, but shifting towards putting pressure on governing bodies to end the surgeries. I came up in this organization called InterACT, and I was a youth in their youth program back in the day, maybe ten to twelve years ago. Back then, it was just five or six of us, and we were in our twenties or younger, and we had a youth coordinator who was intersex, and most of us were still so afraid to be publicly intersex that our activism entailed writing blogs under pseudonyms. That was ten years ago. Then, I elevated to become the youth coordinator of that program, and the program expanded, and I think because I just didn't give a fuck if people knew I was intersex. I didn't use a pseudonym. As I got older, I was more vocal and more out there, and I know that helped inspire younger people to feel like they can come up and talk about this stuff publicly. I eventually worked for InterACT full time, in a few different capacities. But their whole thing is legal and finding laws— and we were losing! And I hate losing. Eventually, when I transitioned out of InterACT, I didn't know what to do for a while with intersex activism, so I gave talks and did my own thing. Then, I called my friends up one day to start an intersex person of colour group, which became the Intersex Justice Project (IJP). I called Saifa (Sean Saifa Wall) and Lynnell (Lynell Stephani Long), two Black intersex friends of mine, and said, "Do you want to start an intersex POC thing," and they were like, "Yeah, let's do it." So that formed in 2016. We were inspired by that first wave of intersex activism that ISNA did back in the day, on the streets. There hadn't been a protest for intersex rights that we knew of since 1996, so we brought that back. We started a campaign against Lurie Children's Hospital in Chicago to shed light on the injustices that occur there to intersex kids still to this day. We did it because I live in Chicago and because also that's the hospital where my surgeries occurred. We built a coalition of people, allies, and friends—a lot of trans allies, especially, and I say that because the first protest in 1996 was with trans allies and intersex people together, which is a beautiful history and it's still like that today. We lean heavily on trans allies and supporters. We had a success this summer[2020], where we got together and got Lurie Children's Hospital to formally apologize and commit to taking steps to ending. They did an immediate moratorium and committed to end intersex genital mutilation long term. That's my style of activism, outside of the nonprofit structure. We started IJP without any grants or nonprofit status. I felt burnt out from working at InterACT. I wanted to be free to do whatever we wanted and say whatever we wanted, and I think that's what has worked for us and for me. We also rely heavily on our friends at InterACT. Saifa was the board president when I worked there, and we still have relationships with them. Like I said at the beginning of our conversation, the intersex community is very small and intimate, so they are not strangers to us. When we are doing campaign work or protests, we are on the phone every day with InterACT and other people. We have allies from the Human Rights Watch. Some who work in the hospitals, some celebrities. We're all on Signal chat. I talked to an Illinois state representative today. I can text her! Basically, that's my style. Bringing a bunch of people together, getting them to call out what's happening behind closed doors at these hospitals, because for thirty years I saw that trying to talk reason into these doctors wasn't working and trying to get the laws changed wasn't working. It's a huge expenditure of time, resources, and energy. I looked around at my community in Chicago who had a bunch of wins when it comes to intense stuff—my friends who created this campaign, to get reparations from the policy department for torture survivors from policy brutality; they won! So I was inspired by their activism, [which was] happening in the streets and through coalition building, to do the same with intersex justice. I always say that I just lift a lot of the best ideas from my friends' movements and campaigns and try to transport them to intersex justice work. What people can do is—there's so much. Number one, get educated and then teach another person—teach one, reach one. There are documentaries and films; there are books. A great website is 4intersex.org, and there are resources on there for how to be allies. There are four ways for how to help us out; it takes people from all walks of life and brings you into the movement. There's a free presentation on that website that you can give to your communities, a Google presentation. Intersex Justice Project has an Instagram [account], and there are links there, including one called "26 Ways to Show Up for Intersex People," which we co-created with InterACT and which is a great jumping off point. And lastly, just call out your local children's hospital. If you have a children's hospital in your area and it's a premium one or known as a great one, chances are they are doing this; they have a clinic where they see intersex patients, and they are doing these surgeries. Take inspiration from IJP, which started out with three people, part-time, volunteering our time, and we were able to amass enough pressure with friends and allies. And by shining the light on what's going on there, we ended up with a hospital changing its policy. Anyone can do that. Figure out what you are best at and do that. Shine a light on what's happening in the hospitals. What are the tools that you have? You could write a press release, donate, paint signs, come to protests. There is always a way that people can plug in; they just have to want to.

K: That's a great list of suggestions, thank you. And thank you for sharing your thoughts on moving beyond the binary in reproduction and parenting life. This was awesome. Take good care.

Chapter 10

"Bring in the Argentine Macho": Feminist Resistances to the Participation of AFAB Trans People in Sexual and Reproductive Rights Activism

Blas Radi and Moira Pérez

Introduction

The recent parliamentary debate in Argentina regarding the legalization of voluntary interruption of pregnancy brought forwards discussions about who are the subjects with the ability to gestate, who should be included in sexual and reproductive rights, and who are the allies in this particular cause. Although proponents of the so-called prolife initiatives (which were defended by the most conservative sections) and proponents of the legal strategies adopted by movements supporting the legalization of voluntary abortion had conflicting aims, in both cases, they assumed that the only ones able to become pregnant (and, therefore, to abort) are women. The latter, identified in Argentina with a green handkerchief, articulated their demands in terms of the human rights of (cis) women, focusing on their dignity, full authority, capacity, and right to decide for themselves and their bodies.

The existence of AFAB (assigned female at birth) trans people evidences that women and people who can became pregnant are not synonymous: on the one hand, because there are women who do not have this ability; on the other, because there are people who are not women and actually gestate and abort. Still, cis feminist organizations and activists often showed enormous resistance to acknowledge this, thus leaving AFAB trans people on the opposite side of any possible alliance. Such tensions, however, were often overlooked or ignored by perspectives that only acknowledged the debate "for" and "against" the legalization of abortion, thus failing to perceive that both positions relied on what we identify as a cisnormative ontology.

Some organizations that converged in the National Campaign for the Right to Legal, Safe, and Free Abortion argued that trans men had demands that were too novel; that they were very few; that they did not participate in the political process in favour of the legalization of abortion; that they could harm the treatment of the project; and, above all, that they wanted to damage women (we will come back to this below).[1] But trans male activists were far from absent in the movement for the legalization of abortion; rather, we interpret this as yet another example of the erasure of trans masculine activism in progressive contexts. Here this erasure comes with an additional twist, whereby a problematic circular logic condemns these subjects to political impossibility: "You are not participating; therefore, you cannot partic-ipate because you are not participating."[2] As a consequence, any alliance with trans men was presented as not very strategic (at best) or as a threat that had to be resisted (at worst). Overrunning the rights of trans men was then seen as an unwanted but necessary consequence of vindicating women's rights.

Of the different projects discussed in the National Congress, only one considered "all persons" as subjects of rights (Exp. 2492-D-2017). The rest referred strictly to (cis) women and in some cases extended its coverage to other "people with ability to gestate in accordance with the Gender Identity Law" (as stated in an additional article in Exp. 230-D-2018, and in the project rationale for Exp. 1082-D-2018). Finally, the draft approved at the plenary session of deputies introduced the formula "woman or person with the ability to gestate" in all its articles. This change in wording, however, was not an expression of a deeper transformation—that is, one able to reach the criteria for political participation, the agenda of social movements, or the definition of the universe of allies.

In this chapter, we will reconstruct the scenario and the terms of the concealed debate between feminist sectors and groups of AFAB trans people. With this objective, we will begin by laying out the Argentine normative framework that describes the very progressive terms of its Gender Identity Law, along with its epistemic and political implications and the limitations of certain interpretations of it. A thorough consideration of this law is central to any understanding of the debates regarding abortion legislation in the country. As a result of important changes in Argentine legislation, where trans people are no longer required to be sterilized in pursuit of legal gender recognition, an increasing number of AFAB trans people are in a position of needing abortion services while being legally recognized as something other than women. With this context in view, we will then specify the legal context regarding abortion and present an array of resources used by feminist groups to exclude AFAB trans people from discussions of the draft bill on voluntary interruption of pregnancy, which we will call "the strategy of anything goes"—that is, a strategy whereby the end justifies the means, even if said means are contrary to the values that allegedly underpin the movement. A brief conclusion will then sum up the itinerary of the chapter and will offer some final considerations about the underlying commitments of feminist positions.

Before starting, it is necessary to make some preliminary clarifications. First, why do we refer to a "concealed" debate? Discussions between feminist sectors and AFAB trans people about the subject of reproductive rights have a long history in our country. An exploration of the literature, however, reveals a profusion of texts by trans AFAB people who respond critically to decisions, practices, and arguments that, although pervasive, are not openly acknowledged by the feminists disseminating them. That means that if we limit our analysis to written sources, we only hear one side of the conversation. To highlight the aspects of the debates that are not found in the literature, we decided to include those feminist positions expressed orally in the context of conferences, social networks, and meetings of political organizations. We do not refer to the authors by name, since our aim is not to denounce them; rather, we are interested in opening a space of encounter for reasons, grounds, and arguments that will push forward the debate on sexual and reproductive rights for all people with the ability to gestate.

Second, if in what follows we occasionally refer exclusively to trans men, it is in order to reflect the historical context of the debates we are reconstructing. Although non-binary and other AFAB trans people are obviously also affected by these policies, in Argentina, the emergence of non-binary activism and organizations is relatively recent. Therefore, the arguments we analyze here were not targeted at other AFAB trans people. Reflecting the historicity of these exchanges is fundamental, particularly considering that what we will call the "novelty" argument—that is, the assertion that the demands of trans people are too novel and, therefore, it is justified not to make room for them—is one of the most common strategies used to discredit trans people and exclude them from constructive political participation.

Conceptual Change, Social Change

In recent years the interactions, habits, and institutions in relation to the ways gender and sex are understood have experienced great transformations all around the world. In many regions, including an important portion of Latin America, the impact and ramifications of such changes have spread throughout the social fabric, eroding the current meaning of those concepts in favour of interpretive resources that better capture the diversity of human experience and are consistent with international human rights law. Numerous national and international regulatory instruments in the region have echoed these transformations, as is the case of Argentina, Colombia, Uruguay, Mexico, and Costa Rica, among others. However, meanings owing to previous conceptions of gender and sex are still alive, even in social movements that promote progressive agendas, including feminist movements. In this chapter, we will refer in particular to the Argentine case and reconstruct its specific regulatory framework and the tensions generated around the legalization of the voluntary termination of pregnancy.

The Argentine Gender Identity Law (Law 26,743) was sanctioned in May 2012. Since then, the country recognizes for every person (a) the human right to gender identity, (b) the right to the free development of personhood according to their gender identity, and (c) the right to be treated in accordance with their gender identity and, in particular, to be identified in this way in the instruments that prove their identity with respect to the registered first name(s), image, and sex (Law 26.742, Art. 1).

This law adopts almost word for word the definition of "gender identity" provided by the *Yogyakarta Principles on the Application of International Human Rights Law to Issues of Sexual Orientation and Gender Identity* (Yogyakarta Principles), according to which

> gender identity is understood to refer to each person's deeply felt internal and individual experience of gender, which may or may not correspond with the sex assigned at birth, including the personal sense of the body (which may involve, if freely chosen, modification of bodily appearance or function by medical, surgical or other means) and other expressions of gender, including dress, speech and mannerisms. (Signatories of the Yogyakarta Principles, *Yogyakarta Principles*)

In practical terms, this definition dismantles gender dogma articulated around sexual difference and the gender binary. Specifically, it implies that (1) sex is not an immediate bodily condition (in fact the law does not refer to "sex" and much less to "biological sex" but to an administrative marker consigned as "sex assigned at birth"); (2) gender does not depend on the sex assigned at birth; (3) genitals are not the essential sign of gender (and there is no essential body marker); (4) gender is not (necessarily) permanent (this means that a person can be registered under a certain gender and eventually not identify with it); and (5) identifying with a gender other than the one assigned is not a disease or an error, but just one possible experience among others. In other words, the definition acknowledges that some people will not identify with the gender assigned at birth, thus doing away with the exceptional character of this experience. The law therefore establishes an administrative mechanism to modify data in identity documents, emphasizing self-determination and not requiring diagnostic accreditations, body scrutiny, or surgical commitments. More importantly for our purposes, this means that Argentina does not establish requirements for forced sterilization as a condition for the recognition of a gender identity different from that assigned at birth (Cabral, "Los géneros").

It is worth highlighting that Argentine legislation does not determine the repertoire of available identity categories. Precisely because it understands that gender is a subjective experience, it leaves this definition free to the experience of each person. It is on this basis that, for example, in November 2018, the civil registry of the province of Mendoza proceeded to the registration of a person leaving blank the field of "sex" in the birth certificate. This has vital implications for reproductive health and rights because it means that Argentina officially recognizes the existence of women who produce sperm, men with the ability to gestate, and people who do not identify as men or women but maintain their reproductive abilities.

Actual Change?

This conceptual change, however, does not seem to have had a correlation in the design of public policies or in the agenda of social movements, which have tended to rely on a cisnormative ontology—that is, an understanding of existence deeply grounded on cisnormativity. Viviane Vergueiro Simakawa describes cisnormativity as a logic based on three fundamental assumptions: 1) the prediscursiveness of sex; 2) the gender binary; and 3) the permanence of gender (Vergueiro Simakawa). Building on her contributions, we conceive cisnormative ontology as a perspective that brings the three assumptions signalled by Vergueiro to the consideration of what kinds of entities exist in the world in relation to their experience of gender and their degree of "realness" (with some being considered real; others, artificial or inauthentic; and others still, inexistent). As a result, cisnormative ontology assumes a universe composed exclusively of cis women and cis men. Its roots run deep in Argentine society and give shape even to initiatives "with a gender perspective" led by feminist movements. As Mauro Cabral explains:

> The absolute ontological dependence of the gender perspective on sexual difference produces an immediate and persistent optical effect: this perspective only "sees" women and men. This optical reduction imposes a strict limit both to the possibility of recognizing the universe of subjectivities that exceeds the gender binary, and to critically addressing the logic that institutes differentiated orders of subjectivity. ("La paradoja transgénero")

Comprehensive sex education (ESI, for its initials in Spanish) offers an interesting example of this phenomenon. In 2006, the Argentine Congress passed a law that establishes that "every student has the right to receive comprehensive sexual education" in all educational institutions of the national territory (Law 26.150, 2016, Article 1). Its contents have been, and still are, a subject of debate. After all, sex, sexuality, and gender, as well as education, constitute social domains disputed by different theoretical perspectives, political positions, and moral and religious regulations.

Some people with conservative religious commitments are strongly opposed to ESI on the grounds that it allows for the infiltration of so-called gender ideology in order to indoctrinate children against the will of their families (CONSUDEC). In fact, the sanction and application of ESI rekindled the dispute between progressive sectors in the state and religious sectors, particularly the Roman Catholic and Neo-Pentecostal churches. The Roman Catholic Church, for instance, resisted the requirements of the law, challenged the curricular guidelines and pedagogical resources of sex education, and edited its own materials through the Superior Council of Catholic Education (CONSUDEC). These resources defend the role of the family as a "natural" educator; the biological anchoring of female and male identities; the roles of women and men arranged by divine authority; and reproductive heterosexuality in marriage as the will of God. Another approach, embedded in the founding positivist tradition of Argentine schooling, equates sexuality and reproduction and confines sex education to the field of biology (Morgade and Alonso; Morgade). Contemporary perspectives on educational sciences and feminism, meanwhile, understand that institutions always educate on sexuality—even if they do not do so willingly or explicitly—and that conscious work on this subject allows them to critically approach institutional life, well beyond the specific contents regarding sexuality (Trujillo). This revision involves a deep restructuring that includes, among other things, the design of curricula and syllabi, the development of equal treatment policies and opportunities for cis women and men, and the elimination of representations, images, and discourses that produce and consolidate gender stereotypes (Morgade).

Currently, comprehensive sex education addresses the axes of body care and health, gender, rights, diversity, and affectivity. Its comprehensiveness covers biological, psychological, social, cultural, emotional, ethical, and legal aspects, which are approached in a transversal way. Where applied, it has had excellent results regarding the dismantling of stereotypes about gender roles and the detection and prevention of child abuse (which is documented to occur primarily within families) (Ministerio de Educación).

Still, although the pedagogical resources of the Comprehensive Sex Education Program have been updated—and its implementation is largely due to the commitment of social movements—they remain within the gender binary and tend to reinforce cisnormative ideals in a rationale that ties gender identity to sexual characteristics. The same can be said about state programs and materials in reproductive health as well as initiatives on this subject born from social movements. Contrary to the definition of "gender identity", in each case the survival of the "natural attitude of gender" is revealed; in short, it is assumed that there are two sexes, two genders, and a link of biological necessity between them (Kessler and McKenna).

Feminist theoretical and political approaches to masculinities share these commitments as well. Their work understands that masculinity is not an essence. It is not defined by biology; it is not embodied in the same way in all men (not all men are equal), and it is not static but historical (it does not mean the same in all ages and cultures) and open to change (and masculinity studies tend to be strongly committed to political programs). Still, the "us" of new and old masculinities—of hegemonic masculinity and antipatriarchal masculinities—seems to always be cis (and mainly heterosexual). The subject being called on to stop occupying leading roles, to stop exercising violence, to call himself feminine, to renounce the privileges of masculinity, and even to stop being male is a cis subject (Bonino; Branz; Volnovich; Bard Wigdor).

On Reproductive Injustices

Current regulations governing abortion in Argentina date from 1921, when the Criminal Code established a regime that penalized women and those who collaborated with them to terminate a pregnancy and considered a set of circumstances in which abortion was not deemed punishable: when practiced by a physician with the consent of the pregnant woman in cases of danger to life, danger to health, or rape, particularly when the victim had a mental health disability (arts. 85 and 86 of the Criminal Code; whether "mental health disability" was an additional circumstance or a condition to access abortion in cases of rape was a matter of extended debate). This means that abortion was established as legal in certain cases, as early as 1921. However, due in large part to the moral veto that falls on this practice, it often remained inaccessible—and still does—even in those circumstances (Bergallo).

In this restrictive environment, discussing abortion requires discussing stigmas, prejudices, clandestine practices, criminal sanctions, and death. But it also involves talking about social movements that since the recovery of democracy in the early 1980s have placed this issue at the centre of public debate and have managed to have impact on different spheres by extending the legitimacy of this practice beyond a legal framework that tends to oppose it. Facilitating access to this practice in repressive contexts, redefining its intelligibility frameworks, and seeking to modernize its legal regime are still some of the most salient efforts of the local feminist movement.

Since 2005, a national coalition called Campaña Nacional por el Derecho al Aborto Legal, Seguro, y Gratuito (National Campaign for the Right to Legal, Safe, and Free Abortion) has managed to position abortion as a matter of public health, social justice, and women's human rights. Regarding the first point, they have emphasized that the complications of unsafe abortions are one of the main causes of "maternal mortality"—in itself a questionable term, since it assumes that all pregnant people are mothers from the moment of conception)[3]—in Argentina (ELA, CEDES, and REDAAS). As for the second, they have shown that the most vulnerable sectors in society are the ones who suffer the most negative consequences of its illegality. In relation to the last point, they have emphasized the idea of (cis) women's rights as human rights, with special focus on their right to decide for themselves and their bodies in relation to their reproductive life (Bergallo).

Recent treatment of the legalization of voluntary termination of pregnancy in the Argentine Congress made public some long-standing discussions about this last point, which may have gone unnoticed for those only attentive to the debate for or against the legalization of abortion. AFAB trans people in Argentina have provided factual, logical, legal, and political reasons that invited policymakers and social movements to reexamine advocacy strategies for reproductive rights; they have highlighted that the category "women" is not exactly equal to "people with the ability to gestate." As mentioned above, there are women unable to become pregnant, and there are people who are not women, and might want or need access to an abortion, as is the case with some AFAB trans people (Cabral, "Caballo de Troya"; Radi "Aborto y varones trans" and "Political Mythology"; Máscolo).

Ironically, resistance from those advocating the right to legal, safe, and free abortion were the first obstacles to this articulation.[4] The motto "women decide, men accompany" served the purpose of pointing at the marginal role of men in the actual practice of abortion (and consequently in the debate) and, ultimately, distinguishing friends from foes. In this scenario, the debate on whether to adopt or not a category that included other subjects capable of gestating must be read as merely one symptom of a much broader discussion central to feminist politics and activism: Who is the subject of reproductive rights? Who is the subject of feminism? What concept of gender should we adopt? Who are allies in this cause? In other words, there was more at stake than just reproductive rights, which explains the pressure against what, at first glance, could seem like a mere change in vocabulary. We would now like to consider some of the arguments that were given at the time, in which these underlying conceptions are made evident. As we shall see shortly, all these arguments seem to have in common a certain license to leave aside fundamental commitments of feminism, which is why we will refer to it as the strategy of "anything goes."

The Strategy of "Anything Goes"

One of the arguments used to keep the language focused on women's rights was to affirm that reproductive policies must explicitly and exclusively refer to women (understanding this, in fact, as cis women) because otherwise (cis) women would not be able to understand the proposal. This would be the case, for example, if we addressed the issue in terms of "people who are pregnant" or "people with the ability to gestate" instead of just referring to "women." This argument was never stated in official documents of feminist organizations or in the media, but it was defended by key figures of the movement during discussions on this topic. The evident (and worrisome) misogyny underlying its premises is such that it should not be dignified with any response.

A similar argument stated that referring to AFAB trans people (for example, saying that abortion is a right of every person with the ability to gestate) "erases women". As in the previous case, this argument is not held openly on official documents or academic papers. Nevertheless, is has been—and still is—frequently used in oral exchanges both in activist and academic environments as well as in social networks and other informal media.[5]

It is not clear to us why the incorporation of certain subjects would necessarily imply the erasure of others. Even if this was the case, this is interestingly ironic, if we consider that John Stuart Mill is often recognized for his contributions to feminism precisely for proposing to use the term "person" in his amendment to the Electoral Reform Project (1867). That is, to replace a gendered term for a universal one, which is exactly what is being questioned here. Mill's proposal, far from erasing women, sought to open a space for participation in civic life and could be incorporated in a long tradition of feminist work oriented to challenge and dismantle the androcentrism embedded in the law—that is, the way in which the law has taken the andros as the model of humanity (Szapuova). By andros, and hence androcentrism, feminist thought has referred not merely to men but rather to a certain model of what a man should be: white, property owner, and holder of social, economic, and political power. This ideal of the human, which Amparo Moreno Sardá has called the "virile archetype," comes back in the form of feminist arguments against the inclusion of AFAB trans people in initiatives, policies, and laws in favour of legal abortion, as will be argued below.

There were also those who considered that the number of AFAB trans people who are affected by these rights violations was negligible compared to the number of cis women. The female majority, therefore, would justify the exclusion of trans AFAB people from the agendas of social movements and the lack of public policies. It is true that all existing reports and statistics on this matter reflect an eloquent choice in statistic samples: 100 per cent of the individuals are cis women. However, existing research does not interrogate the gender identity of the subjects because they assume that any individual with the ability to gestate is a woman. In the context of such informational erasure (Bauer et al.), this is not a result of research but a tacit premise—a premise which, again ironically, reinforces the idea that maternity is a space reserved for women, or perhaps even the female space par excellence. But even if the majority argument were true, we can still question what would be the harm of incorporating other subjects who also experience similar phenomena into the coverage of rights (for a more thorough analysis of this argument, see Radi, "Injusticia reproductiva").

Yet other sectors have maintained that since the subject of feminism is women, those who should be incorporated into the cause of abortion are trans women. In relation to AFAB trans people, on the contrary, some activists consider that they have no viable demands, since (1) if they use their reproductive abilities, they would be women, and (2) if they were men, they would be sterile and/or have no fertile sexual practices and/or would be outside the scope of feminism. Thus, although we are aware that there are pregnancies by people who are not women,[6] the beliefs of these groups about reproductive processes present them as experiences unique to women and, as we pointed out earlier, tend to identify women with reproduction (which seems suspiciously close to patriarchal representations of femininity). So even though trans women do not have the ability to gestate (yet), organizations such as Amnesty Argentina point to "the barriers that women, trans women and girls face to legal abortion today." This could be due to a resistance to recognize (trans) men as subjects of abortion, or to recognize trans men as men, or a combination of both.

Once again, an epistemic obstacle prevents us from seeing beyond women when we consider reproduction, and vice versa. The alleged inability of anyone other than (cis?) women to experience pregnancy (and its interruption) in their own body was taken as self-evident and was also seen as a determining factor in the legal status of abortion. For instance, the slogan "if men could get pregnant, abortion would be legal" resonated strongly during the 2018 debate, which transcended the legislative chambers and seized the mass media, social networks, jobs, families, friends, etc.

Committed to antipatriarchal ideals, many feminist activists questioned men who "sought the spotlight" and called on them to merely follow women's lead. Thus, the slogan "women decide, men accompany" in fact served as code for identifying allies. For AFAB trans people, in contrast, it was a Catch 22: It offered the possibility of having a voice in the public arena, but a voice that could not articulate its own demands.

These difficulties of political articulation were reflected in the hearings of experts who were selected to present (in favour or against legalization) in the National Congress before the vote of the representatives: Of the more than eight hundred speakers, only two were trans men, and no other trans AFAB people were invited. Leaders of the National Campaign for Legal, Safe, and Free Abortion requested fellow activists to "bring in the Argentine macho,"[7] privileging the voices of heterosexual cis men.

Each of these arguments refers to different realms of the debate on the subject of abortion rights. Whereas some of them consider the linguistic dimension of the demands, legislation, and policies, others also involve the epistemic and political dimensions of participation and research. All of them seem to have in common a certain leniency to affirm positions that have historically been challenged by feminist movements, which is why, as we suggested above, we are inclined to affirm that when it comes to advocating the legalization of abortion, the ends justify the means or, to put it more bluntly, "anything goes."

Nowadays, due to AFAB trans activism, the term "people with the ability to gestate" has been brought into the debates and legislative projects. This, however, has not been followed by the incorporation of AFAB trans people in deliberative processes, be it as political subjects or as epistemic peers.

Conclusion

In this chapter, we have attempted to show some important changes in the understanding of gender in Argentina, their translation into a legal framework, and some of the resistances they still generate—specifically those due to the limitations inherent in what is known as the "gender perspective." We focused on the resistances at stake in the field of (non) reproductive rights and looked into their legal regulation as well as, and more importantly, their cultural articulations. In this framework, we examined some of the arguments used in the Argentine context to obstruct the participation of AFAB trans people in the processes of designing legislation and public policies on voluntary abortion.

An analysis from an Argentine perspective provides necessary insight into what can happen with mainstream feminist approaches to sexual and reproductive rights in a context where trans activism has been able to ensure progressive legislation regarding gender identity. This is evident in the arguments listed above as well as in others we have addressed elsewhere.[8] Although rights are not scarce goods (the possession of which, in the hands of one group, would necessarily imply depriving another group of them), important sectors of feminism have considered it necessary to defend the right to abortion as a right of women—to defend it from AFAB trans people. The arguments used in this process, some of which we described above, show how the resistances at play in feminist movements make evident, in a most surprising and unexpected way, the survival of misogynist, patriarchal, and androcentric commitments where one least expects it.

Endnotes

1. Although this legislative debate impacts all people who were assigned female at birth, many organizations have focused their critiques on the needs of trans men, to the exclusion of other AFAB trans people.

2. We thank Kori Doty and A.J. Lowik for pointing this out.

3. We thank Mario Pecheny for bringing this to our attention.

4. Although we recognize that feminist thought, theory, and practice are manifested in diverse ways both within Argentina and globally, we are focusing here on the debate around abortion legislation in Argentina, which has predominantly occurred within a landscape of feminist thought that centres cisgender women's experiences.

5. See, for example, the discussion regarding an article titled "Abortion Is a Right for Trans Men and All Gestating Bodies" (Críticas cítricas).

6. Apart from the news on pregnant men that circulated worldwide, Argentine media has also featured news on local trans men. See "Nació la hija..." and "Seguridad social...".

7 . This is a literal quote from a key figure of the movement, cited in an internal communication of the National Campaign; as we clarified in the beginning, however, our interest here is not to impugn the individual, but rather to expose how this expression encapsulates and evinces a number of underlying assumptions on gender,

identity, the body, and political participation in the struggle for sexual and reproductive rights.

8. See for example Pérez and Radi; Radi, "Political Mythology."

Works Cited

Amnistía Internacional. *El acceso al aborto en Argentina. Una deuda pendiente. Aportes al debate sobre derechos sexuales y reproductivos.* Buenos Aires: Amnistía Argentina, 2017. Web. 10 October 2019.

Bauer, Greta, et al. "'I Don't Think This Is Theoretical; This Is Our Lives': How Erasure Impacts Health Care for Transgender People." *Journal of the Association of Nurses in Aid Care*, vol. 20, no. 5, 2009, pp. 348-61.

Bard Wigdor, Gabriela. "Aferrarse o soltar privilegios de género: sobre masculinidadeshegemónicas y disidentes." *Península*, vol. 11, no. 2, 2016, pp. 101-22.

Bergallo, Paola. *Aborto y Justicia Reproductiva.* Editores del Puerto, 2011.

Bonino, Luis. "Masculinidad hegemónica e identidad masculina." *Dossiers feministes*, vol. 6, 2003, pp. 7-36.

Branz, Juan Bautista. "Masculinidades y ciencias sociales: una relación (todavía) distante." *Descentrada*, vol. 1., no. 1, 2017, p. e006.

Cabral, Mauro. "Caballo de Troya (Transmasculinidades, derechos sexuales y derechos reproductivos)." *Emancipaciones feministas en el siglo XXI*, edited by Gleidys Martínez Alonso and Yanet Martínez Toledo, Ruth Casa Editorial & Editorial Ciencias Sociales, 2010, pp. 175-88.

Cabral, Mauro. "La paradoja transgénero." *Sexualidad, ciudadanía y derechos humanos en América Latina: un quinquenio de aportes regionales al debate y la reflexión*, edited by Carlos Cáceres et al. Sexualidad y Desarrollo Humano & Universidad Peruana Cayetano Heredia, 2011, pp. 97-104.

Cabral, Mauro. "Los géneros de la noticia." *Pagina 12*. 22 February 2013. Web. 10 October 2019.

CONSUDEC. *Aportes para la implementación del Programa de Educación Sexual Integral.* Santillana, 2013.

Críticas Cítricas. "El aborto es un derecho para las mujeres. M-U-J-E-R-E-S Las leyes de identidad de género borran a las mujeres" (Abortion is a right for women. W-O-M-E-N Gender identity laws erase women). *Facebook*. 20 July 2019, www.facebook.com/criticas citricasradfem/photos/a.253488488582939/4260056 24664557/. Accessed 30 Oct. 2021

ELA, CEDES, and REDAAS. "Las cifras del aborto en Argentina. El debate exige datos precisos y evidencia empírica de fuentes válidas." 1 Mar. 2018, *Redaas.org*. Accessed 24 Oct. 2021.

Kessler, Susan, and Wendy McKenna. *Gender. An Ethnomethodological Approach*. University of Chicago Press, 1985.

Máscolo, Tomás. "El aborto es un derecho para hombres trans y todo cuerpo gestante." *La Izquierda Diario*, 7 August 2018. Web. 10 October 2019.

Ministerio de Educación. "Lineamientos curriculares para la educación sexual integral." Programa Nacional de ESI." *Ministerio de Educación*, 2018, www.argentina.gob.ar/sites/default/files/lineamientos_0. pdf. Accessed 30 Oct. 2021.

Moreno Sardá, Amparo. *El arquetipo viril protagonista de la historia. Ejercicios de lectura no-androcéntrica*. Ediciones La Sal, 1986.

Morgade, Graciela, and Graciela Alonso, eds. *Cuerpos y sexualidades en la escuela. De la "normalidad" a la disidencia*. Paidós, 2008.

Morgade, Graciela. *Toda educación es sexual*. La Crujía, 2011.

"Nació la hija del primer hombre embarazado de la Argentina" (Daughter of Argentina's First Pregnant Man Was Born). *La Nación*, 19 Dec. 2013, www.lanacion.com.ar/sociedad/nacio-la-hija-del-primer-hombre-embarazado-de-la-argentina-nid1649316/. Accessed 30 Oct. 2021.

Pérez, Moira, and Blas Radi. "Algunos casos de mala praxis retórica y crímenes de lesa argumentación en los debates contemporáneos sobre aborto." *Relámpagos*, 14 May 2018, www.aacademica.org/moira.perez/45. Accessed 30 Oct. 2021.

Radi, Blas. "Aborto y varones trans." Presentation at event Varones y Aborto. Decisión de ellxs, conquista de todxs, Centro Cultural de la Cooperación, Buenos Aires, 3 July 2014.

Radi, Blas. "Political Mythology on Abortion and Trans Men." *Sexuality Policy Watch*, 29 May 2018. sxpolitics.org/political-mythology-on-abortion-and-trans-men/18439. Accessed 30 Oct. 2021.

"Seguridad Social de Argentina otorgó asignación por embarazo a varón trans." ILGA-LAC, 10 Feb. 2010, www.ilga-lac.org/seguridad-social-de-argentina-otorgo-asignacion-por-embarazo-varon-trans/. Accessed 30 Oct. 2021.

Signatories of the Yogyakarta Principles. *Yogyakarta Principles on the application of International Human Rights Law to issues of Sexual Orientation and Gender Identity*, 2007, yogyakartaprinciples.org/principles-en/. Accessed 30 Oct. 2021.

Signatories of the Yogyakarta Principles. *The Yogyakarta Principles Plus 10*, 2017. yogyakartaprinciples.org/principles-en/ypl0/. Accessed 30 Oct. 2021.

Szapuova, Mariana. "Mill's liberal feminism: Its legacy and current criticism." *Prolegomena: Journal of Philosophy*, vol, 5, no. 2, 2006, pp. 179-91.

Trujillo, Gracia. "Pensar desde otro lugar, pensar lo impensable: hacia una pedagogía queer." Educação e pesquisa, vol. 41, 2015, pp. 1527-40.

Vergueiro Simakawa, Viviane. *Por inflexões decoloniais de corpos e identidades de gênero inconformes: uma análise autoetnográfica da cisgeneridade como normatividade*. M.A. Dissertation, Programa Multidisciplinar de Pós-Graduação em Cultura e Sociedade, Instituto de Humanidades, Artes e Ciências, Universidade Federal da Bahia (Brazil), 2015.

Volnovich, Juan Carlos. "Viejas y nuevas masculinidades." *Mujeres y varones en la Argentina de hoy*. Siglo XXI, 2017.

Chapter 11

Lessons Learned from Researching Non-Binary Reproduction

Olivia Fischer

In this chapter, I identify the lessons that I have learned while undertaking my thesis research and reflect on their importance to me as a researcher as well as to the growing field of trans-inclusive reproductive healthcare research and literature. I focused my thesis on the conception, pregnancy, and birth narratives of five AFAB (assigned female at birth) non-binary individuals. Throughout this book chapter, I share some of my findings and the lessons I learned, consolidated from both the academic literature as well as from the stories of the people who participated in my study. Specifically, I explore the themes of transphobia, cisnormativity, and heteronormativity, the importance of gender-affirming care, identity disclosure, and the balancing of transition and reproduction goals. I identify the lessons that I learned along the way, particularly with regards to the importance of social support, reasons for optimism, and the amount of work that remains to be done. I conclude by providing my reflections as a researcher. My intention is for this chapter to act as a knowledge translation tool and bring my academic findings into community. Ideally, this effort will provide a useful resource for those who do not fit within the gender binary and are considering pregnancy. Additionally, I hope that those who are providing reproductive healthcare to non-binary individuals can learn from this chapter and work to improve the care they provide. For those looking for specific recommendations for providers, Alexis

Hoffkling, Juno Obedin-Maliver, and Jae Sevelius have an excellent paper that covers this topic. It is open source and freely accessible online.

Methods and Participants

I adopted a qualitative, narrative approach to collect the reproduction narratives of five non-binary individuals (Riessman). Participants were recruited through purposeful sampling, specifically snowball and convenience sampling. Essentially, I asked community contacts to distribute my recruitment materials to those whom they thought might be eligible and interested. All five participants identified as non-binary; one participant, Alex (not his real name), identified as both trans-masculine and non-binary. Four participants identified as queer and one participant, Sol, identified as pansexual. Sol identified as multi-racial, and the remaining four participants identified as white. Participants had between one to three children, all of whom they gave birth to. At the time of the interview, all participants were located in Canada, and their ages ranged from thirty-one to forty-four. Using unstructured interviews, I simply asked each participant, "What is your story of conception, pregnancy, and birth?" After I had transcribed each interview and written each individual's reproductive narrative, I sent it back to each participant. I then asked them if there was anything that they would like to add, change, or delete to ensure that the story I had written accurately captured their experiences.

Transphobia, Cisnormativity, and Heteronormativity

Transphobia, cisnormativity, and heteronormativity are embedded within our institutions, policies, and practices and have significant implications for trans people building their families (Oswald, Blume, and Marks; Pyne, Bauer, and Bradley). Transphobia has resulted in children being taken away from trans parents in custody battles, trans people being denied biological children through sterilization during gender-affirming surgeries, and numerous barriers erected for trans people accessing assisted reproduction and adoption services (James-Abra et al.; Lowik, "Reproducing"; Pyne, Bauer, and Bradley; Stotzer, Herman, and Hasenbush). Cis- and heteronormativity assume families are comprised of a heterosexual, cisgender man and woman, coupled together, along with their heterosexual, cisgender offspring (Downing; Oswald, Blume, and Marks). Within this culture of cis- and hetero-normativity, the dominant birth narrative maintains that only cisgender women conceive, carry, and give birth to their children, which erases the experiences of trans individuals who conceive and birth their children. These social systems lead to assumptions about the links between body parts, gametes, gender, sex, sexual orientation, and family configurations (Epstein). Therefore, non-binary individuals are often put in a position of having to defend, explain, and protect themselves, their families, and their reproductive choices (Epstein). Furthermore, navigating spaces traditionally considered as women-only, such as birthing wards and obstetric and gynecologic doctors' offices as a non-binary person frequently means that their bodies, identities, and family configurations are misrecognized and mis-understood (Epstein). This institutional erasure and relentless need for self-advocacy can be exhausting and isolating (Bauer et al.; Ellis, Wojnar, and Pettinato). Given these challenges, the very act of having a family as a trans person can be understood as an act of empowerment (Hoffkling, Obedin-Maliver, and Sevelius).

The topic of transgender reproduction has received minimal investi-gation within the academic literature (Charter et al.; Ellis, Wojnar, and Pettinato; Light et al.; Obedin-Maliver and Makadon; T'Sjoen, Van Caenegem, Wierckx). When the topic has been broached, it has relied on binaristic understandings of gender (focused largely on trans men) and often overlooks the experiences and identities of non-binary individuals (Charter et al.; Light et al; Obedin-Maliver and Makadon; T'Sjoen, Van Caenegem, Wierckx). One participant in my study, Alex (non-binary and transmasculine and thirty-two years old) commented on this erasure: "Our culture is even just now starting to acknowledge trans people, binary trans people, even that they exist and are maybe worth respecting. Non-binary people, society doesn't really have a box for that; it's considered to be unserious, and it's not respected, generally" (Fischer).

While I was reviewing the relevant literature, it became apparent just how little there is available in terms of research, resources, and support for non-binary people seeking pregnancy. This informational erasure (lack of available resources and knowledge of non-binary pregnancy) provides tangible evidence for the existence of transphobia, cisnormativity, and heteronormativity (Bauer et al.). The individuals who participated in my study commented on the lack of information that was available to them during their own reproductive journeys and reported an eagerness to contribute to my research in hopes of providing non-binary folks who pursue reproduction with more resources (Fischer). I am extremely grateful for their time and willingness to have shared their personal and nuanced stories. Their stories challenge binaristic understandings of gender, counter the status quo, and illuminate the impact of cis- and heteronormativity on their reproductive experiences.

Gender-Affirming Care

Unsurprisingly, having access to gender-affirming care during and after pregnancy is incredibly important and positively impacts trans people's experiences of perinatal care (Hoffkling, Obedin-Maliver, and Sevelius). Very simply, gender-affirming care means respecting a person's gender identity, partnership and parenting configurations, and body (Hoffkling, Obedin-Maliver, and Sevelius). Within the limited literature, trans individuals have reported overwhelming negative experiences while navigating reproductive care (Berger et al; James-Abra et al.). Participants in numerous studies have reported a lack of representation on clinical documentation, being misgendered and/or deadnamed (referring to a patient by their birth name instead of their chosen name) by staff and service providers, having to consistently combat heteronormative assumptions, and in extreme cases, being refused services (James-Abra et al., and Hoffkling, Obedin-Maliver, and Sevelius). Given the aforementioned challenges, many trans individuals express a desire to remain out of traditional hospital settings when undergoing pregnancy and birth, opting for midwifery care instead (Ellis, Wojnar, and Pettinato). Three out of the five participants in my thesis research opted for midwifery care (Fischer). Regardless of their choice to be supported by a midwife or OB-GYN through their reproductive care, each participant commented on how access to, or unavailability of, gender-affirming care influenced their experiences (Fischer). For example, Finley, a thirty-one-year-old non-binary person said: "You have the right to define your own experience and to advocate for the things that are important for you. Talk to other non-binary and trans people who've had pregnancies to find out what's been awesome for them and what hasn't worked ... what kind of care providers they would recommend because care providers are one of the most important things you can have."

By not making assumptions, using gender neutral forms as well as correct pronouns and names, being knowledgeable about possible testosterone use, gender dysphoria, and chestfeeding, and mirroring the language that a person uses to describe their body, healthcare providers can make a dramatic impact on non-binary people's experiences of reproductive healthcare (Hoffkling, Obedin-Maliver, and Sevelius).

Social Support and Community

Talking with the five non-binary individuals in my study, I learned how imperative social support is when pursuing parenthood. Each person I interviewed stressed how important having community was, either in its absence or existence (Fischer). Within the literature on transmasculine pregnancy, loneliness and isolation are unfortunately consistent themes (Charter et al.; Ellis, Wojnar, and Pettinato; Light et al.; Hoffkling, Obedin-Maliver, and Sevelius). One factor that contributes to this sense of isolation is arguably the hypergendering that accompanies pregnancy and the potential challenges of finding supportive community while pregnant (Light et al.). For example, Sam, a thirty-three-year-old non-binary person said: "Do what you can to find community, particularly before you give birth.... It can be hard to find people with shared experiences after. Having people who can block and get in-between you and the gendering of pregnancy is really helpful.... My partner went and got me nursing bras, so I didn't have to navigate the maternity store."

Three participants who participated in my research study mentioned that they were able to find community online when they were unable to access trans-specific social support in their day-to-day life (Fischer). Sam mentioned that while there are often groups for new parents, these are often very gendered and ill-equipped to support non-binary folks. Two participants noted that they faced additional difficulties in finding community due to their respective decisions to use they/them pronouns for their child (Fischer). This decision continued their need to self-advocate, explain, and defend their choices even after their pregnancy. Having community that is understanding and supportive can greatly ease the transition to parenthood, and this seems especially true for non-binary people based on the experiences shared by my participants (Goldberg and Smith; Semyr et al.).

Identity Disclosure

Pregnancy is often a challenging and overwhelming time regardless of gender identity. Adding the layer of resisting and navigating the gendered, social ideas that surround pregnancy can greatly complicate the experience. For example, Sol, a forty-four-year-old non-binary person who participated in my study, said:

> It's okay to give yourself the breathing space you need, whether you're pregnant or not, but even more so when your body is doing a very challenging thing. The easiest pregnancy in the world is still hard ... you get to give yourself as much slack as you need to get through that in the best way that you can ... think carefully about where you want to spend your energy. Pregnancy is gendered ... I would tell them to think very carefully about where they want to spend their energy because it is extremely difficult to get away from the gender and the pregnancy.

Non-binary individuals who are pregnant or considering pregnancy are often challenged to make decisions about disclosing their gender identity, if they are in a position to make such a choice. The people who participated in my thesis research made various choices about disclosing their non-binary identity to their healthcare providers. Two participants had access to gender-affirming care and, therefore, freely disclosed their gender identity to their healthcare providers. For two others, these choices were dependent on context and were often informed by a fear that asking for gender-affirming care would further complicate their experiences and create barriers to accessing care (Fischer). Finally, one participant did not disclose their gender identity at any stage during their reproductive care, recognizing that there was already a lot going on. Perri, a thirty-four-year-old non-binary person, gave the following advice to other non-binary individuals navigating pregnancy:

Just do what you need to do. In a certain way, being pregnant is a very common experience, and in another way, there are parts of it that are not as common so whatever you need to do to have it feel more comfortable for you. Just do that and just be comfortable making a new trail for certain things if you need.... There are other people who have gone before us, so find some of those people who have written about their experiences.

Balancing Transition and Reproductive Goals

In general, transgender people have a range of goals regarding transition. Therefore, it follows that some non-binary folks may become pregnant at various times relative to potential social, medical, and surgical components of a transition. However, during this decision-making process, there may be a tension between pursuing reproduction and transition goals (Hoffkling, Obedin-Maliver, and Sevelius; T'Sjoen, Caenegem, and Wierckx; Verlinden). This tension exists for a variety of reasons. A contributing factor is that the social discourse that entangles concepts of femininity and womanhood with the act of pregnancy have resulted in some trans individuals feeling that pregnancy is incongruent with their gender identity (Verlinden). As a result, reproduction may feel at odds with their transition goals. Additionally, there has been substantial gatekeeping regulating transition and reproduction both medically and legally (Verlinden). Access to gender-affirming procedures has been regulated by how well that individual adheres to cis- and heteronormative narratives. By rejecting their so-called previous gender and reproductive capacity, trans people are seen as more legitimate and more aligned with cisnormative ideals and, therefore, are given greater access to gender-affirming procedures (Lowik, "Betwixt"; Doussa). Therefore, for trans men, loss of reproductive function was often seen as the price to pay for transitioning (T'Sjoen, Caenegem, and Wierckx). Furthermore, laws have historically (and presently in some jurisdictions) regulated reproduction as a component of transition, requiring a trans person to fully transition, erasing their reproductive capacity, in order to receive legal gender recognition (Verlinden). These laws have relied on and maintained the gender binary system and have refused to consider non-binary ways of being (Lowik, "Betwixt"; Sharpe). Through the erasure of the so-called previous gender, attempts have been made to erase trans people's reproductive capacities as well (Lowik, "Betwixt"; Sharpe; Doussa).

This is a complex issue that was seen in the narratives of my thesis participants. Within their stories, there was often a tension between pursuing their reproductive and transition goals. They were often challenged to balance their mental health, gender dysphoria, and reproduction goals. They grappled with decisions around sequencing testosterone use and conception, top surgery and chestfeeding, and consciously considering their gender presentation to increase their chance of safety.

There is a dearth of systematic studies examining best practices regarding reproduction and testosterone use (WPATH). It is recommended that non-binary and transmasculine individuals wishing to become pregnant stop taking testosterone in order to restore menses and fertility (Light et al.). However, some trans individuals become pregnant while taking testosterone (Jarin; Light et al.; T'Sjoen, Caenegem, and Wierckx), suggesting that in some cases, menses and fertility can be maintained during testosterone use. Other trans people have irreversibly lost their reproductive function as a result of prolonged hormone use (Light et al.; Doussa).

Furthermore, there is also a tension between electing to have top surgery and desires to chestfeed an infant in the future (MacDonald et al.). Four participants in my study commented on how their intention to nurse their child influenced the decisions they made about top surgery (Fischer). Although chestfeeding may be possible after certain forms of chest reconstruction, including the use of a supplementary feeding system, it is not possible to determine this prior to attempting to chestfeed (Light et al.; Obedin-Maliver and Makadon). Three participants chose to wait to pursue top surgery until their child(ren) had weaned and stopped nursing (Fischer). Two of those three commented that they had intentionally held off on pursuing gender-affirming top surgery because of their reproductive goals (Fischer). These findings are mirrored by MacDonald et al. in their paper on transmasculine individuals' experiences with lactation and chest-feeding. It is critical that care providers, particularly those providing medical support for those who are transitioning, be aware of and discuss reproductive goals with their patients prior to intervention, to assist trans individuals to make informed, empowered decisions.

Although this tension between reproduction and transition goals is predominantly relevant to medical transition, there is also a tension when pursuing social transition. Some may elect to postpone social transition to avoid the difficulties of navigating the deeply powerful cisnormative, heteronormative assumptions that accompany pregnancy (Hoffkling, Obedin-Maliver, and Sevelius). Four participants in my study commented on the considerations they made around being out and pregnant such as thinking about their own safety, the safety of their children, and how the potential impact of being out may impact their quality of care (Fischer). That non-binary people are making both transition-related and reproductive decisions on the basis of fear and concerns over their safety both within and outside of healthcare spaces is a depressing reality and highlights the pervasive discrimination and transphobia many non-binary individuals are surrounded by.

Reasons for Optimism

Although there are undeniable challenges that accompany non-binary pregnancy as a result of heteronormativity, cisnormativity, and transphobia, there are also wonderful gifts that come with stepping outside of these social norms (Pyne, Bauer, and Bradley). Moving away from normative gender identity and family configurations, trans individuals may be particularly well positioned to develop parenting and partnering relationships that do not rely on gendered norms when constructing divisions of labour, for example. Despite cisgender, heterosexual couples' best intentions to equally distribute tasks, they often fall into more traditional gender roles after they become parents (Koivunen, Rothaupt, and Wolfgram). The flexibility afforded by a non-binary identity may also allow for increased flexibility to invent parenting roles and create dynamic parenting and family configurations (Petit, Julien, and Chamberland; Pyne, Bauer, and Bradley).

Although heteronormativity and cisnormativity are persistent social forces, the strength and resilience of the five individuals who participated in my thesis research shone through (Fischer). The very act of choosing to have a child as a non-binary individual is an act of empowerment (Hoffkling, Obedin-Maliver, and Sevelius). Trans communities are overcoming institutional erasure, structural barriers, and are creating the space to make their families (Bauer et al.). Anecdotally, it seems that there is increasing visibility of trans and non-binary individuals and that an increasing number are choosing to conceive their families. I am hopeful that slowly, reproductive health-care providers will continue to unlearn heteronormative, cisnormative assumptions and increase the inclusivity of their services.

Researcher Reflections

Like many graduate students, I bounced between topics before I landed on my final area of focus. Initially, I was set on researching the experiences of cisgender, queer women pursuing reciprocal in vitro fertilization (IVF). However, after sifting through the academic literature, I recognized that the voices of cisgender, queer women were surprisingly well represented (Hayman et al; Roth), and I wanted my research to elevate the voices unheard, the experiences unseen. After informally consulting some trans folks, I shifted my focus to trans reproduction and parenting and eventually refined my topic to explore non-binary conception, pregnancy, and birth.[1]

Similar to how my research focus shifted, so did my gender identity. One of the most profound and personal lessons I have learned through undertaking this project is the discovery of my own non-binary identity. I began this project identifying as a cisgender, queer woman but as I became increasingly immersed within trans community and was met with acceptance, kindness, and mentorship, I was able to understand that my own experience of gender better fits within the non-binary ethos. Through my own gender journey, I have learned firsthand the barriers that come with challenging one of society's most deeply embedded cultural concepts: the gender binary. It is exhausting to constantly have your identity challenged, erased, and denied.

While undertaking this research, I also learned the sobering reality of how pervasive and insidious transphobia is. Living in Vancouver, and working in non-profit, social justice organizations, I have predominantly been surrounded by people who emphasize inclusion and actively respond when they witness discrimination. However, any time I exited this bubble, I was astounded by people's inability to grasp my thesis topic and their continued inflexibility to comprehend trans reproduction and non-binary identities. As a researcher, this disappointment does not even touch the painful experiences of those who have lived this transphobic discrimination, particularly in relation to creating their families. Prior to undertaking this research, I was naïve to the vast amount of work that needs to be done, not only in trans reproduction but in trans-inclusion more generally. It is essential that we begin to disentangle gender from the biological acts of conception, pregnancy, and birth and change policies to allow greater freedom and flexibility for non-binary people to biologically create their families.

Endnotes

1. I wish to offer a personal thank you to both Kori and A.J., the editors of this book, as they both influenced my research in profound ways. Kori helped me refine my research topic, and A.J. assisted me to be more inclusive of non-binary folks. I am incredibly grateful to both of them for having made small comments that resulted in large changes. Thank you.

Works Cited

Bauer, Greta, et al. "'I Don't Think This is Theoretical; This is Our Lives': How Erasure Impacts Health Care for Transgender People." *Journal of the Association of Nurses in AIDS Care*, vol. 20, no. 5, 2009, pp. 348-36.

Berger, Anthony, et al. "Pregnant Transmen and Barriers to High Quality Healthcare." *Proceedings in Obstetrics and Gynecology*, vol. 5, no. 2, 2015, pp. 1-12.

Charter, Rosie, et al. "The Transgender Parent: Experiences and Constructions of Pregnancy and Parenthood for Transgender Men in Australia." *International Journal of Transgenderism*, vol. 19, no. 1, 2018, pp. 64-77.

Doussa, Henry von, Jennifer Power, and Damien Riggs. "Imagining Parenthood: The Possibilities and Experiences of Parenthood Among Transgender People." *Culture, Health & Sexuality*, vol. 17, no. 9, 2015, pp. 1119-31.

Ellis, Simon A., Danuta M. Wojnar, and Maria Pettinato. "Conception,

Pregnancy, and Birth Experiences of Male and Gender Variant Gestational Parents: It's How we Could Have a Family." *Journal of Midwifery & Women's Health*, vol. 60, no. 1, 2015, pp. 62-69.

Epstein, Rachel. "Space Invaders: Queer and Trans Bodies in Fertility Clinics." *Sexualities*, vol. 21, no. 7, 2018, pp. 1039-58.

Fischer, Olivia. *Transmasculine and Non-Binary Reproduction: Stories of Conception, Pregnancy, and Birth.* 2020, University of British Columbia, MA thesis.

Goldberg, Abbie E., and Julianna Z. Smith. "Stigma, Social Context, and Mental Health: Lesbian and Gay Couples Across the Transition to Adoptive Parenthood." *Journal of Counseling Psychology*, vol. 58, no. 1, 2011, pp. 139-50.

Hayman, Brenda, et al. "Lesbian Women Choosing Motherhood: The Journey to Conception." *Journal of GLBT Family Studies*, vol. 11, no. 4, 2015, pp. 395-409.

Hoffkling, Alexis, Juno Obedin-Maliver, and Jae Sevelius. "From Erasure to Opportunity: A Qualitative Study of the Experiences of Transgender Men Around Pregnancy and Recommendations for Providers." *BMC Pregnancy and Childbirth*, vol. 17, no. 2, 2017, pp. 7-20.

James-Abra, Sarah, et al. "Trans People's Experiences with Assisted Reproduction Services: A Qualitative Study." *Human Reproduction*, vol. 30, no. 6, 2015, 1365-74.

Jarin, Jason. "The Ob/Gyn and the Transgender Patient." *Adolescent and Pediatric Gynecology*, vol. 31, no. 5, 2019, pp. 298-302.

Koivunen, Julie M., Jeanne W. Rothaupt, and Susan M. Wolfgram. "Gender Dynamics and Role Adjustment During the Transition to Parenthood: Current Perspectives." The Family Journal, 17.4 (2009): 323-328.

Light, Alexis D., et al. "Transgender Men Who Experienced Pregnancy After Female-to-Male Gender Transitioning." *Obstetrics & Gynecology*, 124.6 (2014): 1120-1127. Web. 23 Nov 2019.

Lowik, A.J. "Betwixt, Between, Besides: Reflections on Moving Beyond the Binary in Reproductive Health Care." *Creative Nursing*, vol. 26, no. 2, pp. 105-08.

Lowik, A.J. "Reproducing Eugenics, Reproducing while Trans: The

State Sterilization of Trans People." *Journal of GLBT Family Studies*, vol. 14, no. 5, 2018, pp. 425-445.

MacDonald, Trevor, et al. "Transmasculine Individuals' Experiences with Lactation, Chestfeeding, and Gender Identity: A Qualitative Study." *BMC Pregnancy and Childbirth*, vol. 16, no. 1, 2016, pp. 1-17.

Obedin-Maliver, Juno, and Harvey J. Makadon. "Transgender Men and Pregnancy." *Obstetric Medicine*, vol. 9, no. 1, 2016, pp. 4-8.

Oswald, Faith F., Libby B. Blume, and Stephen R. Marks. "Decentering Heteronormativity: A Model for Family Studies." *Sourcebook of Family Theory and Research*, edited by Vern L. Bengtson, et al. SAGE, 2005, pp. 143-65.

Petit, Marie-Pier, Danielle Julien, and Line Chamberland. "Negotiating Parental Designations among Trans Parents' Families: An Ecological Model of Parental Identity." *Psychology of Sexual Orientation and Gender Diversity*, vol. 4, no. 3, 2017, pp. 282-95.

Pyne, Jake, Greta Bauer, and Kaitlyn Bradley. "Transphobia and Other Stressors Impacting Trans Parents." *Journal of GLBT Family Studies*, vol. 11, no. 2, 2015, pp. 107-26.

Riessman, Catherine. *Narrative Methods for the Human Sciences*. Sage Publications, 2008.

Roth, Amanda. "(Queer) Family Values and Reciprocal IVF": What Difference Does Sexual Identity Make?" *Kennedy Institute of Ethics Journal*, vol. 27, no. 3, 2017, pp. 443-73.

Semyr, Louise, et al. "In the Shadow of Maternal Depressed Mood: Experiences of Parenthood During the First Year After Childbirth." *Journal of Psychosomatic Obstetrics and Gynecology*, vol. 25, 2004, pp. 23-34.

Sharpe, Andrew N. "A Critique of the Gender Recognition Act 2004." *Bioethical Inquiry*, vol. 4, 2007, pp. 33-42.

Stotzer, Rebecca L., Jody L. Herman, and Amira Hasenbush. "Transgender Parenting: A Review of Existing Research." *UCLA: The Williams Institute*, 2014, escholarship.org/uc/item/3rp0v7qv. Accessed 25 Oct. 2021.

T'Sjoen, Guy, Eva V. Caenegem, and Katrien Wierckx. "Transgenderism and Reproduction." *Current Opinion in Endocrinology*, vol. 20, no. 6, 2013, pp. 575-79.

Verlinden, Jasper. "Transgender Bodies and Male Pregnancy: The Ethics of Radical Self-Refashioning." *Machines: Bodies, Genders and Technologies*, edited by Michaela Hampf and Maryann Snyder-Korber, Universitatsverlag Winter, 2012, pp. 107-36.

World Professional Association for Transgender Health (WPATH). "Standards of Care for the Health of Transsexual, Transgender, and Gender Nonconforming People." 7th version, 2011, pp. 1-120.

Chapter 12

Bloody Cycles: One Indian/Pakistani Feminist Perspective on Menstrual Health

Taq Kaur Bhandal
ਤਕਦੀਰ ਕੋਰ ਭੰਡਾਲ

Trigger warning: Colonialism leading to the establishment of North America

Introduction

Menstrual cycles, or mahwari ਮਾਹਵਾਰੀ (Punjabi), can be considered the fifth vital sign of health along with breath, pulse, blood pressure, and temperature (Hendrickson-Jack). I suggest that for body, mind, and spirit, mahwari cycles can be tapped into as tools of self-care and collective care. For instance, I interpret mahwari cycles as fractals of the natural seasons of our planet: winter/ period, spring/preovulation, summer/ovulation, and autumn/PMS (Bhandal). From an Indian/Pakistani feminist perspective, I understand the vitality of my uterus to reflect the health of the earth, universe, and humanity across intersecting relations.

In this chapter, I offer one Indian/Pakistani feminist perspective to explore diverse discussions of mahwari health. From my subjective position, I share three examples from the archives of knowledge about mahwari cycles from wide geographies (not so ironically written in English, with some Punjabi words sprinkled in), which have been braided with and resisted the modern-colonial-capitalist-hetero-patriarchal-extraction-based world in nuanced ways. For the purposes of this chapter, I briefly summarize the teachings as 1) Sikh-Punjabi gender equity and mahwari, 2) Māori mahwari power, and 3) African American sacred blood. This chapter is based on an assumption that all research is necessarily subjective to the positionality and experiences of the researcher and authors.

Theoretical-Spiritual-Embodiment Framework

I am so incredibly grateful for the genealogy of authors, activists, and menstruators across our planet whose teachings have informed this chapter and have informed who I am as a writer and researcher right now. Their philosophies and ways of being—what I consider my Indian/Pakistani feminist perspective—make up the delicious daal of ideas that ground me as a mahwari health researcher in this moment in time and space.

Indigenous caregivers and scholars of decolonial praxis have taught me that I am connected to land and all more-than-human beings (Arvin, Tuck, and Morrill; Battiste; Tuck and Yang). One analysis suggests that land holds the deep pain and trauma inflicted by processes such as settler colonialism. I interpret that many of us also survive, thrive, and are nourished by the land. Many wise teachers, some of which are cited above, remind me that I cannot decolonize without reimagining my relationship to land.

Researchers who raise critical race theory, postcolonialism, and intersectionality—all theoretical/practical cousins—teach me to really deconstruct and reconstruct the social relations I use to create binary divisions between my relatives and relations on Earth (Andreotti; Bhambra; Crenshaw; Dhamoon; Hill Collins; Thobani). The siyaneh (Elders) and my peers who write about these complex theories also provide explanations, ideas, and commiserations about the experiences of people of colour in the racialized, modern, and colonial world. Some of the constructed binaries that scholars alert me to and that I experience in my life include binary/non-binary, brown/white,

religious/secular, us/them, Kaur/Singh, straight/queer, Indian/
Pakistani, male/female, woman/man, citizen/immigrant, Indigenous/
settler, and Sikh/any other South Asian religion.

I find that perhaps the most problematic I come across on a daily
basis is the binary of human world/nature. I hear this binary invoked
when I hear phrases like "I feel like going out into nature this weekend!"
Interestingly, the scholars referenced above also point to the concept of
binaries as stemming from the severing of body-mind-spirit to yield the
body/mind binary (as Cartesian dualism). Scholars of critical race
theory, postcolonialism, and intersectionality point to noticing the
ways that human existence is reflective of a constellation of identities,
not just two options.

Finally, gender diverse practitioners of generative somatics offer the
awareness of finding life/death balance through the body-spirit-mind
connection through a social justice lens (Generative Somatics). In brief,
generative somatics "is a mind/body methodology that builds embodied
leadership to align our personal and collective practices with our
principles and to heal from trauma and internalized oppression"
(Generative Somatics). They carry on lineages of ancestral knowledge
that centre everyday intention setting in body-mind-spirit. For
instance, practitioners support clients and movement leaders to
understand ourselves as a part of human consciousness. As such, I
understand that they put forth the notion of humans as spiritual beings
who exist in relation to the fluctuating conditions inside to outside of
the body. I find that a generative somatics frame can be tapped into
through paying close attention to all mahwari cycles. All of these
teachings inform the perspective of this chapter.

Globalization, Approaches to Mahwari Cycles, and Balancing Pluralism

In the last two-hundred-plus years, approaches to mahwari cycles have
evolved with ongoing globalization. In the case of my current home,
Canada, I understand that healthcare approaches to mahwari health
went through a bottleneck effect starting in the 1800s which carried
through until today (Ahenakew; Duran and Duran; Sousa Santos).
According to written and oral hxrstories, many diverse worldsenses
about mahwari healing went underground, and biomedicine became

the main model of health in the newly formed country. Drawing on the teachings of Temitope Adefarakan and Oyèrónké Oyewuní, I use "worldsense" instead of "worldview" here to disrupt the privileging of the visual and of sight. The authors state that worldsense is a more inclusive way of describing the conception of the world by people across the globe.

In the last fifty years, approaches to mahwari cycles have been informed by the advent of mahwari technologies such as fertility awareness apps for smart phones, access to safe abortion services, the birth control pill and additional exogenous hormones, as well as a wide range of reusable mahwari supplies such as mahwari cups (Hendrickson-Jack). The shifts and access to reproductive technologies have been largely informed by feminist and/or healthcare movements around the world (Armstrong and Pederson; Bose; Hill Collins; Prior; Sen). Notably, LGBTQ researchers and allies have evolved important considerations of deconstructing sex, gender, as well as the naturalness and essentialism of bodies (Butler; Cheung et al.; Dzubinski and Diehl; Jhappan; Tudor).

At the same time, some scholars find that twentieth-century approaches to health in general, and mahwari cycles specifically, are also intertwined with modern processes, such as capitalism, colonialism, and heteropatriarchy (Ahenakew; Bobel). Notably, in my experience and research, I find that ancestral practices can often become overshadowed by "modernity's shine" (Andreotti 24). In this chapter, I suggest that Indian/Pakistani feminist perspectives can emphasize a balance of pluralistic healing methods for pelvic health, which can have synergistic effects on our approaches to mahwari cycles in the coming years.

I suggest that there has been an epistemic erasure of mahwari health knowledge that has been traditionally passed on by Indigenous peoples, witches, shamans, femmes, as well as non-binary, gender diverse, and two-spirit members of our ancestral and contemporary communities (Sousa Santos). I should note here that your body is your choice. Whatever measures you want to or feel like you need to take in order to feel your most healthy self are all good. However, I strongly believe in working with ancestral medicines, such as prayer, whole plants, massage, stretching, and meditation, which can greatly complement modern biomedicine, and together they can produce emergent effects on mahwari health.

For mahwari health today, I find that more and more people who menstruate are being empowered to understand their own mahwari cycles and those of the collective as connections to spirit and land. I notice in my own practice and research that there is a growing shift away from understandings of periods and cycles as something to be stigmatized, managed, hated, and hidden away (Bobel).

Reclaiming Ancestral Mahwari Knowledges

According to the teachings I have received, in Latin-based languages, hormones called estrogen, progesterone, and testosterone, the pollinating hormones, manoeuvre through bodies giving signals to regenerate cells, influence emotions, respond to stress, wake us up, and detoxify (Hendrickson-Jack; Prior). At the same time, I understand that the mind has the possibility to analyze using language that uplifts positive thoughts about mahwari and use the embodied experiences of cycles to stay in the here and now, the present moment (Generative Somatics; Kaur Singh). In this way, I propose the health of our body and mind are connected and influenced by both our embodied experience of, and thoughts about, mahwari cycles.

For me, the spiritual aspects of the mahwari cycle are a rich source of knowledge and healing. For instance, in ancestral scriptures of Sikhism, the uterus, vagina, cervix, and the additional facilitators of mahwari cycles are considered grounding energetic centres of the body that bridge life, death, and being. In Sanskrit-based languages, the word "yoni" is used to refer to a pelvic energy centre. In many lineages around the world, I have also come across the metaphor and reality of the four seasons of mahwari cycles: new moon/period/winter, waxing moon/preovulation/spring, full moon/ovulation/summer, and waning moon/PMS/autumn (Bhandal). From my understanding, people who do not identify with the process of mahwari or who are in various states of perimenopause and menopause (e.g., dosing gender-affirming hormones, taking the birth control pill for polycystic ovaries syndrome, fibroids, or endometriosis management, and aging) can still use practices that come with each of the four seasons of mahwari cycles. Rather than, or in addition to, using the body changes as a sign, one can use the moon cycle as a guide.

No matter where one's ancestors are from geographically or the knowledge one chooses to be drawn towards, there are healers who have continued to pass on many pluralistic approaches to mahwari cycles. However, given the current global conditions of modernity, I am especially interested in surfacing solidarities in approaches to mahwari cycles from Indigenous peoples' communities on Turtle Island (North America) and the Global South, Middle World (Ansary), and Pacific Islands (or whichever geographic words you would like to use!). There is much to be written about European ancestral perspectives, such as Wicca, and their applicability to going beyond the binary, although they are out of the scope of this chapter. I look forward to future rich conversations and sharing of practices that generate solidarities across the globe.

In this chapter, I suggest that through the spread of colonialism, heteropatriarchy, and capitalism across the globe, the power of mahwari as a source of wisdom has been historically diminished and made binary. In a world that continues to experience polarization, political unrest, and planetary pollution, reclaiming our ancestral mahwari knowledges seems to be more important than ever.

Methods

In this section, I use gendered pronouns attuned to my own interpretation of my life and experiences of mahwari. I have written this chapter in English, which I learned by being conceived and growing up in suburban towns close to Vancouver, Canada. My family comes from the region that is now modern-day India/Pakistan, a place that has been caught in the middle and ripped apart by many social binaries. I identify as a Sikh-Punjabi second-generation immigrant and a daughter of farmers in Metro Vancouver on Coast Salish Territory.

You might also notice that, where possible, I try not to use gender binary English words—such as male/female, man/woman, and masculine/feminine—to talk about mahwari, unless using a direct quote from an author who has used these binary terms. Instead, I aim to use gender diverse language to represent every person's unique body-mind-spirit. I have also loosely set up the chapter according to the writing standards of qualitative methodologies in academia (Gunaratname; Hesse-Biber). At the same time, I draw on diverse

Indigenous research inquiries, such as storytelling and oral histories—to uncover a piece of the mahwari archives (Battiste; Chilisa; Wilson et al.).

I envision this chapter to feel like a conversation. There are a lot of perspectives that are not shared in this chapter, and I know they are so important to furthering global mahwari health and menstrual equity movements. Feel free to reach out to me through any means possible in the present day or the future, especially if a particular line or passage is touching your heart centre, giving you insight, making you feel unsettled, and/or if you have a totally different story than me.

One Perspective on Sikhism, Mahwari, and Gender Equity

In mainstream discourse, I find it is often assumed that many religions view mahwari as some kind of blight or impurity. In particular, through current iterations of globalization, a narrative has emerged of people identified as young women of colour being sent to cold huts to bleed out their periods (Bobel). Although this may be the case in some families and something important to be interrogated, I think it's important to really think through the call to once again save the so-called poor South Asian and African women (the subaltern). This time of scarcity-based activism tends to take the form of donating money or buying pads and tampons saturated with harmful chemicals. At the same time, there is a very real wave of menstrual activism taking shape around the globe (Bobel). For instance, recently in the current borders of India, over five million women protested their exclusion from specific spiritual sites by forming a three-hundred kilometre human wall (Thiagarajan). In this section, I offer interpretations of Sikhism that celebrate mahwari cycles and shake up commonly held binaries in and of the South Asian diaspora.

As one of the newest religions in world history (only the youthful age of about five hundred), Sikhism broke the trajectory of heteropatriarchal interpretations of scriptures (Aneja). For instance, an Amritsari (orthodox) Sikh of any sex or gender is suggested to not cut any of their body hair. At the beginning, the founders of Sikhi (of all genders) also viewed the menstruating body as a positive, essential part of society. Wisdom from researchers like Nikky-Guninder Kaur Singh explores the early texts of Sikhism and highlights how mahwari was no longer "stigmatized as pollution" (92). She then goes on to say:

We recognize the crimson flow as a
visual celebration of the life-giving
power of blood shed by women
the fertile flow weaves tissues in the womb
regenerating limbs, organs, mind, consciousness, and spirit (83)

Here, Kaur Singh analyzes scriptures such as the *Bictra Natak* and *Guru Granth Sahib* that, in her view, celebrate the myriad ways that mahwari connects humans to the abundance of the cosmos and to parent Earth. The author posits that Sikhi goes beyond the binary by modelling how mahwari cycles can reproduce not only a new human life, mahwari but also the self and collective spiritual consciousness.

Although many South Asian ancestors lived in a gynocratic, gender fluid society, through the evolution in the modern world, Sikhism tends to now be practiced in binary ways in many parts of the world (e.g., men sit on one side of the gurdwara and women on the other, or only men can perform kirtan). These and other troubling symptoms of heteropatriarchy beg the question, "How the fuck did we get here?" Like all cycles of the planet, shifts and adaptations are continuing to happen. In the belly of the colonial beast, UK's oldest Gurdwara (Sikh Temple) in Shepherd's Bush launched a new period policy (Rana). The Gurdwara is now offering free period products in bathrooms, providing public education to reduce stigma, and hosting workshops on mahwari health. Moreover, adaptive activists—like Harnaam Kaur and their stance on polycystic ovaries syndrome (GSN News) and Durga Gwade Studio and their stance on gender diversity (Mehra)—help to evolve the liminal edges of binary mahwari health thinking in diverse South Asian diaspora through art, philosophy, and creative flows.

Some Māori Wisdom on Mahwari

Through the activism and resiliency of diverse Indigenous nations and communities across the world, old ways of tending to mahwari health are being revitalized. It should be noted that Indigenous peoples are incredibly pluralistic and diverse. When I invoke the phrase "Indigenous peoples," I am referring to the multitude of First Peoples across the planet. At the same time, there are commonalities shared through mahwari health that often serve as a reminder of the inter-connections and sharing of knowledge. For instance, in some events and ceremonies held by members of Musqueam, Squamish, and Tsleil-Waututh communities in Coast Salish lands, people on their periods do not touch ceremonial objects or participate in some rituals because they may be considered to be highly energetically charged during mahwari winter (Allen). One analysis suggests that for people who menstruate, periods can be a time of solitude, inner work, journeys, and channeling the increase in energetic flows into creative outlets (Bhandal).

On this note, journalist and researcher Marino Harker-Smith shares some of their knowledge on Māori mythologies on the energetics of periods/mahwari winter:

> Māori women are brought up with the knowledge that when they are bleeding, they must abstain from tasks such as tending to food gardens, or gathering kaimoana [food from the sea]. The misconception is that this is a sign of women being unclean and pollutant, but this chapter will argue, it is in fact because ... menstrual blood is powerful and potent... The key point was the restrictions were self-imposed in order to claim space for themselves and provide a welcome reprieve from the daily demands of community living.

In the excerpt above, one analysis suggests that people who men-struate would typically not participate in specific ceremonies for reasons of rest rather than repression. The author writes how this process involved self-awareness and "self-imposition" of boundaries from "daily demands." In this way, Harker-Smith implies that in some communities people who experience mahwari cycles are revered for their ability to pass through many divine dimensions, the connection to which is especially potent during periods/mahwari winter. In the following section, I elaborate on this point using some African American knowledges on mahwari that I have come across in recent years.

Some African American Knowledges on Mahwari

In North America on Turtle Island, chattel slavery and the transatlantic slave trade inflicted an enormous "soul wound" (Ahenakew; Duran and Duran; Reynolds; Walker). In the material world, for several hundred years, many people from the African diaspora have been cut off from their lineages and mahwari healing traditions due to the intergenerational impact of slavery. Moreover, Alexis Pauline Gumbs finds African diasporic communities can often be pathologized to experience higher rates of fibroids, death during childbirth, and period poverty due to structural racism and colonization. Despite inter-generational trauma, I understand that many African diasporic healers in the United States and Canada are reclaiming and revitalizing ancestral mahwari practices. Omolewa Jennifer Thedford, a placenta alchemist is one such person. She shares the following: "In my community I want to restore the culture of birth.... I found that healing the womb individually and collectively was the missing link.... I also started practicing placenta encapsulation which comes from our [parent], grand[parent], to the first [parent]." Reminiscent of the Māori viewpoints written about in the previous section, she continues:

The awareness, the beauty, the messages that come through our blood, I like to call that information super-highway, because our blood just carries wisdom, it carries knowledge, it carries our ancestors inside of it ... during our period we are more sensitive and able to connect to other dimensions through dreaming and altered states of consciousness.... I compare it to the mycelium.

According to one definition, mycelium is a complex network connection between all fungi that helps ground all beings into dirt and supports the planetary detox process (Fricker et al.). The research suggests that it is the largest known organism on Earth (Fricker et al.). Adrienne Maree Brown, a pleasure activist, also holds out mycelium as a metaphor and model for how we as humans can connect with each other in non-binary ways:

We have to embrace our complexity. We are complex. While many of us articulate a yearning for a more simple life, we continue practicing complexity as our evolutionary path.... I have grown an appreciation for simplicity, while also understanding that I enjoy it as a visitation—that being in a complex life is actually intriguing and delicious to my system. And that I have to understand that it isn't just my own complexity at work, but everyone I am in relationship with creating an abundance of connections, desires, interactions, and reactions. (53)

Based on their writings, I suggest that mahwari blood is like mycelium. It allows me to communicate with the people around me ("I need space"; "I'm in pain"; "Can you bring me snacks?"), and I find it to be part of the collective detox process. The teachings above also suggest that mahwari winter can be a time for things to go underground, turn inwards, and hibernate in our power.

Summary

In this chapter, I share many ancestral teachings that inform my particular Indian/Pakistani feminist perspective on mahwari cycles. The authors and healers cited in the previous pages share insights that continue to shift my everyday experiences of mahwari cycles as well as how I engage in mahwari health research and practice and how I coexist with every being on the earth.

From my perspective, the original scriptures of Sikhism promote acceptance of mahwari as a life source. Māori traditions illuminate the notion that mahwari winter/periods can be a particularly powerful expression of energy. Finally, I find that African American diasporic healing philosophy provides instructions on how to listen and learn from mahwari blood. Overall, in the offering above, I shared three entry points into my own Indian/Pakistani feminist perspective on mahwari—a worldsense that attempts to engage in mahwari health praxis beyond the binary.

Works Cited

Ahenakew, Cash. *Towards Scarring*. Musagetes, 2019.

Allen, Paula Gunn. *The Sacred Hoop: Recovering the Feminine in American Indian Traditions*. Beacon Press, 1992.

Andreotti, Vanessa. *Actionable Postcolonial Theory in Education*. Springer, 2011.

Andreotti, Vanessa de Oliveira et al. "Towards Different Conversations About the Internationalization of Higher Education." *Comparative and International Education/Éducation Comparée et Internationale*, vol. 45, no. 1, 2015, p. 2.

Aneja, G. *Great Sikh Women*. Unistar, 2007.

Ansary, Tamim. *Destiny Disrupted: A History of the World through Islamic Eyes*. PublicAffairs, 2009.

Armstrong, Pat and Ann P. Pederson. *Women's Health: Intersections of Policy, Research, and Practice*. 2nd edition. Canadian Scholars' Press, 2015.

Arvin, Maile, et al. "Decolonizing Feminism: Challenging Connections between Settler Colonialism and Heteropatriarchy." *Feminist Formations*, vol. 25, no. 1, 2013, pp. 8-34.

Bannerji, Himani. *The Dark Side of the Nation: Essays on Multiculturalism, Nationalism and Gender*. Canadian Scholars' Press, 2000.

Battiste, Marie, editor. *Living Treaties: Narrating Mi'kmaw Treaty Relations*. Cape Breton University Press, 2016.

Bhambra, Gurminder K. "Postcolonial and Decolonial Dialogues." *Postcolonial Studies*, vol. 17, no. 2, 2014, pp. 115-121.

Bhandal, Taqdir. *Self-Care Down There: An All Genders Guide to Vaginal Wellbeing*. Simon & Schuster, 2020.

Bharathi Chandran, Rachelle. "Navigating Healthcare as a Dalit, Non-Binary Person with Debilitating Social Anxiety." *Medium*, medium.com/skin-stories/navigating-healthcare-as-a-dalit-non-binary-person-with-debilitating-social-anxiety-aa378490e144. Accessed 29. Nov. 2019.

Bobel, Chris. *The Managed Body: Developing Girls and Menstrual Health in the Global South*. Palgrave Macmillan, 2019.

Bose, Ashish. "From Population Control to Reproductive Health: Malthusian Arithmetic." *Indian Journal of Medical Research*, vol. 124, no. 2, 2006, p. 213.

Brown, Adrienne M. *Pleasure Activism: The Politics of Feeling Good*. AK Press, 2019.

Butler, J. *Gender Trouble: Feminism and the Subversion of Identity*. Routledge, 1999.

CeMCOR. "Cramps and Painful Periods." www.cemcor.ca/resources/ topics/cramps-and-painful-periods. Accessed 31 Oct. 2021.

Cheung, Ada S. et al. "Non-Binary and Binary Gender Identity in Australian Trans and Gender Diverse Individuals." *Archives of Sexual Behavior*, vol. 49, no. 7, 2020, pp. 2673-81.

Chilisa, Bagele. *Indigenous Research Methodologies.* Sage Publications, 2012.

Collins, Patricia Hill. *Black Feminist Thought: Knowledge, Consciousness, and the Politics of Empowerment.* Routledge, 2002.

Cooper, Melinda. "The Law of the Household: Foucault, Neoliberalism and the Iranian Revolution." *The Government of Life: Foucault, Biopolitics, and Neoliberalism*, edited by Vanessa Lemm and Miguel Vatter, Fordham University Press, 2014, pp. 29-58.

Crenshaw, Kimberlé. "Mapping the Margins: Intersectionality, Identity Politics, and Violence against Women of Colour." *Violence against Women: Classic Papers*, edited by R.K. Bergen et al. Pearson Education, 2005, pp. 282-313.

Dhamoon, Rita. "A Feminist Approach to Decolonizing Anti-Racism: Rethinking Transnationalism, Intersectionality, and Settler Colonialism." *Feral Feminisms*, vol. 4, 2015, pp. 20-37.

Duran, E., and B. Duran. *Native American Postcolonial Psychology.* State University of New York Press, 1995.

Dzubinski, Leanne M. and Amy B. Diehl. "The Problem of Gender Essentialism and Its Implications for Women in Leadership." *Journal of Leadership Studies*, 2018.

Fricker, Mark D. et al. "The Mycelium as a Network." *Microbiology Spectrum*, vol. 5, no. 3, 2017, pp. 23-44.

Garza, Kelly. "Diy Vaginal Steam." *Steamy Chick*, www.steamychick. com. Accessed 16 Jan. 2019.

Generative Somatics. "Our Strategy." *Generative Somatics*, generativesomatics.org/our-strategy/. Accessed Nov. 29 2019.

GSN News. "Harnaam Kaur: I Don't Give a Shit About Gender Stereotypes." *GSN News*, www.gaystarnews.com/article/harnaam-kaur-world-pride-gender-stereotypes/. Accessed 29 Jan. 2020.

Gumbs, Alexis Pauline. "'We Can Learn to Mother Ourselves': A

Dialogically Produced Audience and Black Feminist Publishing 1979 to the Present." *Black Women's Writing Revisited*, no. 22, 2008, pp. 39-73.

Gunaratnam, Yasmin. *Researching 'Race' and Ethnicity: Methods, Knowledge and Power.* Sage Publications, 2003.

Harker-Smith, Marino. "Potent Not Pollutant: Exploring Menstruation in the Māori World." *N8vdaughter*, n8vdaughter.wordpress.com/2016/02/29/potent-not-pollutant-exploring-menstruation-in-the-maori-world/. Accessed 29 Nov. 2019.

Hendrickson-Jack, Lisa. *The Fifth Vital Sign: Master Your Cycles & Optimize Your Fertility.* Fertility Friday Publishing Inc., 2019.

Hesse-Biber, Sharlene. "Feminist Approaches to in-Depth Interviewing." *Feminist Research Practice: A Primer*, 2014, pp. 182-232.

Hill Collins, Patricia, and Sirma Bilge. *Intersectionality.* Polity Press, 2021.

IM With Periods. "Instagram Profile." *Instagram*, IM With Periods, www.instagram.com/imwithperiods. Accessed 29 Nov. 2019.

Jhappan, R. "Post-Modern Race and Gender Essentialism or a Post-Mortem of Scholarship." *Studies in Political Economy*, vol. 51, 1996, pp. 15-63.

Kaur Singh, Nikky-Guninder. *The Birth of the Khalsa: A Feminist Re-Memory of Sikh Identity.* SUNY Press, 2005.

Lock, Margaret, and Vinh-Kim Nguyen. *An Anthropology of Biomedicine.* John Wiley & Sons, 2010.

Mehra, Sanchi. "In Conversation with Durga Gawde: An Artist, Activist and Drag King." feminisminindia.com/2020/10/19/durga-gawde-an-artist-activist-and-drag-king/. Accessed 31 Oct. 2021.

Melamed, Jodi. "The Spirit of Neoliberalism: From Racial Liberalism to Neoliberal Multiculturalism." *Social Text*, vol. 24, no. 4, 2006, pp. 1-24.

Naepi, Sereana. "Indigenous Feminisms: A South Pacific Perspective." *Canadian Graduate Journal for Social Justice*, vol. 1, 2016, pp. 1-10.

Prior, Jerilynn C. "Apply the Precautionary Principle Concerning Combined Hormonal Contraception Use in Adolescents." *Women's*

Reproductive Health, vol. 3, no. 2, 2016, pp. 113-16, doi:10.1080/232 93691.2016.1196086.

Rana, Yudhvir. "London's Oldest Gurdwara to Launch Period Policy." *The Times of India*, timesofindia.indiatimes.com/city/chandigarh/ londons-oldest-gurdwara-to-launch-period-policy/articleshow/ 67462462.cms. Accessed Nov. 29 2019.

Sen, Gita. "Progress of the World's Women 2015–2016: Transforming Economies, Realizing Rights." *Global Social Policy*, vol. 16, no. 1, 2016, pp. 94-96, doi:10.1177/1468018115624314a.

Thedford, Omolewa Jennifer. "Sacred Period Rituals." *Sisters of Flow Podcast*, edited by De'Nicea Hilton, 2017.

Sousa Santos, Boaventura de. *Epistemologies of the South: Justice against Epistemicide.* Routledge, 2015.

Thiagarajan, Kamala. "Millions of Women in India Join Hands to Form a 385-Mile Wall of Protest." *NPR*, www.npr.org/sections/ goatsandsoda/2019/01/04/681988452/millions-of-women-in- india-join-hands-to-form-a-385-mile-wall-of-protest. Accessed 29 Nov. 2019.

Tuck, Eve, and K. Wayne Yang. "Decolonization Is Not a Metaphor." *Decolonization: Indigeneity, Education & Society*, vol. 1, no. 1, 2012, pp. 1-40.

Tudor, Alyosxa. "Im/Possibilities of Refusing and Choosing Gender." *Feminist Theory*, vol. 20, no. 4, 2019, pp. 361-380.

Valverde, Mariane. *The Age of Light, Soap, and Water.* McClelland and Stewart, 1991.

Walker, James W. St G. "Black Confrontation in Sixties Halifax." *Debating Dissent: Canada and the Sixties*, 2012, pp. 173-192.

Wilson, Shawn, et al. "Double Perspective Narrating Time, Life and Health." *AlterNative: An International Journal of Indigenous Peoples*, vol. 16, no. 2, 2020, pp. 117-25.

Chapter 13

Case Study: Rowan's Experience Freezing Their Sperm

A.J. Lowik

I first met Rowan in early July 2018, when they volunteered to be a participant in my dissertation research study. Although my master's thesis research and subsequent activism was focused squarely on trans and non-binary people's access to abortion services, my goal with my dissertation was to expand the focus to include all facets of trans and non-binary peoples' reproductive lives, health, and decision making. I wanted to explore not only how trans and non-binary people experience healthcare in British Columbia, when aspects of their reproduction were involved, but also what practices, discourses, and logics informed their decision making in this area of their lives—it is difficult to know which tense to use, here, as I'm currently analyzing and writing my dissertation into a report that I will defend in front of a committee in a few months' time, so this is very much a project in process. But I digress and intentionally move away from a tangential yet related conversation about queering/trans-ing temporality. I was (am?) eager to unpack the complex entanglement between gender and reproduction in trans and non-binary people's lives. What role, if any, did their understanding of gender norms generally, and their own genders specifically, play in the reproductive choices they made and, conversely, what role, if any, did their reproductive capacities or desires play in their construction and formation of their gender identities? How and when were trans people developing a sense of procreative consciousness? Procreative consciousness speaks to the cognitive and emotional awareness that one can use their reproductive capacities for the purposes of creating new humans both with the aim of parenting or as surrogates, egg and sperm donors, etc. (Berkowitz). Armed with my long list of research questions and equipped with Joan Scott's advice that lived experience narratives are useful in shedding light on underlying hegemonic structures that allow certain experiences to be lived in the first place, I set out to recruit participants for my study.

I had originally intended to recruit twenty participants, ten from the Greater Vancouver Area and ten from the West Kootenays, although I ultimately ended up with fourteen participants in total. This was due to two factors. First, the decision by the Greyhound bus company to stop all service in Western Canada meant that my traveling back and forth to the West Kootenays from my home in Vancouver became impossible both logically and financially. Second, at fourteen participants, I had reached a kind of saturation—that is, the vast majority of the fourteen participants were white, thirty-something, and assigned female at birth (AFAB) non-binary people, sociodemographic characteristics that match my own. I had intentionally set aside the remaining spots for folks who might have had different stories to share, who were somehow different from most of my sample. I had hoped to hear from more Indigenous folks, more people of colour, and more folks assigned male at birth (AMAB) to amplify the voices of those whose stories are frequently marginalized or underrepresented in this field of study. I reached out to folks I knew already in the community, distributed recruitment materials to organizations and agencies serving these prospective participants and attended local events and drop-ins in both locations to listen and learn and to see if anybody else might be keen to get involved in my study. My own positionality and relationship to power and privilege—coupled with the diversity of reproductive experiences associated with female assigned bodies as compared to the relatively few reproductive possibilities for folks with male assigned bodies, along with countless other factors I am sure—meant that my sample remained relatively homogeneous despite these efforts. I elected to stop recruiting at fourteen rather than filling the six remaining spots with participants whose positionalities were already well represented in the sample. My method involved both initial interviews with all fourteen, followed by a participatory photography exercise where each was instructed to create, or select from their existing collections, photographs that related to the theme of the research; it ended with a follow-up interview where those photographs were elicitation tools on which we could delve further into their reproductive lives, health, and decision-making processes. I ended up with twenty-eight interview transcripts and 119 photographs.

One of those fourteen participants was Rowan, a white, mid-thirties assigned male at birth non-binary person. Although Rowan doesn't use "AMAB" to describe themselves personally, they have given me permission to use this language in my writing as a way to create intelligibility about the body they were born into and how they related to their sex assignment at the time of their participation in my research. Rowan was living in the Greater Vancouver Area at the time that we connected. My field notes written after our initial interview remind me of the following: "Rowan arrived in style—they looked beautiful, dressed all in black. They have newly formed breasts that they pointed out to me right away, and they were glowing and radiant." Rowan had only just recently accessed gender-affirming hormone therapy at the time of our initial interview, and they were feeling optimistic about the impact it was already having on their body and their mind. Although Rowan thoughtfully shared stories and insights into everything from their childhood to how their gender informed their art, it is Rowan's experience accessing fertility preservation technologies that I wish to detail here.

For Rowan, having a genetically related child was important and something that they indicated wanting for themselves "always, and [my partner] felt the same way early on in our relationship." The couple had considered their fertility and parenting options long before Rowan came out as non-binary and started accessing gender-affirming medical care—adoption among them but also surrogacy, in which they could use some combination of the genetic material each was able to produce in order to have a child who would be genetically connected to them both. When Rowan started thinking about taking hormones, the need to thoughtfully consider these options had a new sense of urgency, as long-term gender-affirming hormone use for folks assigned male at birth has negative consequences on their future fertility. Rowan was fortunate—by their own account and based on the existing literature on trans people's experiences of health care which suggests that this exceptionally rare (Bauer et al.; Grant et al.)—to have "a great team of physicians around me that advised me." They continued:

> I knew that I needed... to store my sperm so that I could potentially have my own children at some point. That was really like—it was a really *weird* and stressful time for me, although I knew that it was important for me to do. It was so weird to wrap my head around the practice of... being a part of something that is often heavily tied to being a man.... So, it was made pretty clear to me that ... once I start taking hormones, even though I started on Spiro for about six months before I started taking estrogen, I wasn't sure that I was going to start taking estrogen. But I started on Spiro... about a year and a half ago, and then I started estrogen about six months after that, been on estrogen for about a year.... So before that, it was about... a year and a half ago, I guess, that I did the, you know, storage process.... It was explained to me that I would basically become infertile, I would be sterile, I would have no chance of... you know, *contributing* my sperm or my genetics to having a child in the future, after being on hormones. And there's always a slight chance that going off of hormones, you could wait and see if it works, but I wasn't really willing to take that risk. (Rowan's emphasis)

For Rowan, the decision when to initiate hormone therapy, which has known fertility impacts, was tangled together with their reproductive desires for genetically related children. However, achieving this reproductive and family-forming goal meant undergoing a fertility preservation process that they understood as socially entangled with a kind of cisnormative masculinity that they ultimately could not relate to. Perhaps not surprisingly, though obviously distressingly for Rowan, the cisnormative (and heteronormative) assumptions embedded into the process of the cryopreservation of semen continued when they arrived for their appointment:

> I went to a fertility clinic, and we had a long discussion with the physician about the options and what, you know, we could do with the sperm later on, and... thankfully my sample was strong enough... thankfully I didn't have to give other samples, because I *hated* the process of doing it, it was so... counter to – it's so wrapped up in the binary, heteronormativity and... it was funny,

because the room that I was in, they were the rooms for like... donations, or like – [I: Specimen collection?]—specimen collection, yeah. Little chair, dark room, it was so small, probably 5 feet by 5 feet, just a tiny room, little tv screen on the wall, and porn magazines and... there was only—obviously, the rooms were designed for men, and... based around the binary, and like I said, heteronormativity, because it was *all* straight porn, except for one magazine, and you know, twenty magazines. And it was just so gross, it was really a gross experience and it wasn't something that I... it was something that I was stressed out about, and then when I got there, I was even more stressed about it, and... [sigh] the physician was pretty good about understanding... our sort of situation, I think they do deal with trans people... probably less with non-binary people, so it was kind of... a bit of a... a discussion to get to the point where she understood that it was a bit different for me, and for us, because I wasn't transitioning *as a trans woman*—because I think a lot of the language at first *was* about that, how she was understand it, that I was a trans woman, and... so, a lot of the advice that she was giving was kind of—but then I had to sort of – but I think they, it was obvious to me that I wasn't the first non-binary that they had spoken to (Rowan's emphasis).

Here, we see Rowan reflecting first on how the physical space and the provided supplies to facilitate their ejaculation and subsequent sperm/semen collection were seeped in assumptions about who would ultimately be using that space—namely cisgender, heterosexual men, where cisgender, gay men were also somewhat anticipated (although perhaps tokenistically, based on the 19:1 ratio of relevant magazines available). Rowan did not see themselves reflected or anticipated in the space and describes the entire experience as affectively gross and emotionally stressful. In addition to cisheteronormativity, however, Rowan's story alerts us to another set of assumptions embedded in this provider's delivery of care, and which arguably are embedded in many sexual and reproductive health care spaces, health care spaces more generally, and our collective social imagination—transnormativity. Transnormativity describes the process whereby we typically only think about trans people in binaristic and medicalized ways (Johnson; Lowik). That is, we assume that trans people all identify along the binary as either trans men or trans women—indeed, a review of the available empirical literature on the broad topic of trans people and reproductive lives is illustrative of this, with the primary focus being on trans men (a few exceptions include Frank; MacDonald; Riggs and Bartholomaeus). We also assume that trans people will access (or at least ought to desire access to) gender-affirming medical interventions in order to 'align' their sexed bodies with their gender identities. It is from this ideology of transnormativity (which is itself reliant on cisnormativity) that the 'born in the wrong body' narrative emerges, where the 'right' body is one where sex and gender, reproductive life and parenting roles all align in predictable (re: cisnormative) ways. In Rowan's story above, it is trans *women* who are anticipated. It was perhaps Rowan's feminine gender expression which resulted in the assumption on the part of the staff that they were specifically a trans woman. Although Rowan's non-binary identity was ultimately understood and respected by the staff they interacted with, and although it was clear to Rowan that the staff had dealt with non-binary clients before, the default/first attempts at trans-inclusive language that they encountered was language that would have been more appropriate for a trans woman than for an AMAB non-binary person, and Rowan's identity was assumed—when it became clear that Rowan wasn't their typical client (i.e. neither a cisgender, heterosexual man nor a cisgender, gay man), the next educated but ultimately incorrect guess was that they were a trans woman – this is transnormativity at work.

I share this small excerpt of Rowan's story here as illustrative of why it is imperative that we expand our thinking about reproduction and parenting beyond the binary. We can see that Rowan's reproductive and gender-affirming care decisions are tangled together and that hegemonic and dominant norms (cis-, hetero- and transnormativities) were embedded in their experience of care. Not only that, we see that these same hegemonic and dominant norms were understood by Rowan as being parts of the social world which they needed to unpack in order to reconcile their reproductive desires with the ways in which the practices needed to fulfilled those desires are conventionally, traditionally, typically (read: cisnormatively) gendered. Rowan reminds us that we ought not to ignore, or contribute to the perpetual erasure of, the reproductive experiences, lives, health, and decision-making processes of trans and non-binary people who were assigned male at birth.

Works Cited

Bauer, Greta, et al. "'I Don't Think this is Theoretical: This is Our Lives': How Erasure Impacts Health Care for Transgender People." *Journal of the Association of Nurses in AIDS Care*, vol. 20, no. 5, 2009, pp. 348-61.

Berkowitz, Dana. "A Sociohistorical Analysis of Gay Men's Procreative Consciousness." *Journal of GLBT Family Studies*, vol. 3, no. 2-3, 2007, pp. 157-90.

Frank, Sarah E. "Queering Menstruation: Trans and Non-Binary Identity and Body Politics." *Sociological Inquiry*, vol. 90, no. 2, 2020, pp. 371-404.

Grant, Jaime M., et al. *Injustice at Every Turn: A Report of the National Transgender Discrimination Survey.* National Center for Transgender Equality and National Gay and Lesbian Task Force, 2011.

Johnson, Austin H. "Transnormativity: A New Concept and its Validation Through Documentary Film about Transgender Men." *Sociological Inquiry*, vol. 86, no. 4, 2016, pp. 465-91.

Lowik, A.J. "Betwixt, Between, Besides: Reflections on Moving Beyond the Binary in Reproductive Health Care." *Creative Nursing*, vol. 26, no. 2, 2020, pp. 105-08.

MacDonald, Trevor. "Lactation Care for Transgender and Non-Binary Patients: Empowering Clients and Avoiding Aversives." *Journal of Human Lactation*, vol. 35, no. 2, 2019, pp. 223-26.

Riggs, Damien W., and Clare Bartholomaeus. "Fertility Preservation Decision Making amongst Australian Transgender and Non-Binary Adults." *Reproductive Health*, vol. 15, no. 181, 2018, pp. 1-10.

Scott, Joan W. "The Evidence of Experience." *Critical Inquiry*, vol. 17, no. 4, 1991, pp. 773-97.

Afterword

A.J.'s Reflection

I came to this work almost by accident, though with a great deal of intention and dedication once I found myself here. My trajectory to being a non-binary instructor and researcher who studies trans people's reproductive lives (culminating in my eminent PhD dissertation defense and the coediting of this important collection) began twelve years ago. At the time, I was finishing my undergraduate degree in sociology and sexual diversity studies at the University of Toronto while working part-time in an abortion clinic in order to pay my way. In the evenings, I was performing as Johnny Class, a suave and debonair drag king, lip syncing to the likes of Frank Sinatra and Tony Bennett, and using my time on stage to explore my increasingly complicated and uncertain gender. Although I didn't have the language of "non-binary" to describe myself yet, I knew that the identity of "woman" was no longer one that I could stretch to fit over my head. So like an ill-fitting sweater, I discarded "woman" in exchange for a liminal but yet undefined in-between place. My shift away from identifying as a woman put me at odds with the employment policy of the abortion clinic I was working in, however. The tension I felt going to work every day as a not-woman in a women-only space prompted me to consider bigger questions about my workplace. How would a pregnant person who identified as something other than a woman experience care within this space? What barriers to abortion care would such a person experience elsewhere in Canada and beyond, in both hospitals and free-standing abortion clinics? Why was identifying as a woman a requirement for employment, if someone like me might be in need of the services on offer? Prompted by these questions (and to be honest by my increasingly unstable mental health that made my continued employment untenable), I left my job and started looking for answers in the form of a master's thesis in sociology at York University. (In retrospect, it was not the best decision in terms of my mental health, as the degree would take me four years and more than one hospitalization to complete, but in the grand scheme of my life, it was an important, life-changing decision nonetheless.)

It was while conducting my thesis research that I began to have a vision of what my future life could be—that I could be trans (specifically non-binary, language I would discover during those four years) and a researcher and that I could ensure trans people's experiences of reproductive life and health were being captured and written about and used to inform institutional policies and practices. I realized that I could both design and conduct research and teach future generations of students. During my undergraduate degree, a sessional instructor named Dr. Dan Irving taught a trans theory and politics course and, in doing so, opened my mind to the burgeoning field of trans studies. In 2019, when I was offered the opportunity to teach Intro to Trans Studies at the University of British Columbia, I reflected on that impactful course. I approached each lecture and assignment with the heartfelt desire to impact even one student in the way that Dr. Irving had impacted me. My ultimate goal as both a non-binary researcher and instructor is to make trans lives more livable, even in a small way. I do this by placing my community at the centre of my work, always. I do this by putting the knowledge produced by my research into action by training abortion providers and other healthcare workers about trans people's needs. I do this by occupying that liminal space between insider and outsider, where I am at all times both a non-binary person, a member of the population that I study and serve, and a researcher, whose position comes with an incredible responsibility and power that I endeavour to yield with the utmost care.

I am thrilled to have coedited this collection with my friend and colleague, Kori Doty, whose perspective I value beyond compare. They remind me always of how important it is to create work that is accessible and that is grounded in the lives of trans people and connected to action. Together, I believe we have created a collection that recognizes the scholarly value of stories told firsthand by folks with no previous experience writing in this way. It is a collection that tethers the theoretical to the accessible and centres non-binary people's experiences while also recognizing that moving beyond the binary is deeply connected to decolonizing efforts, to antiracist activisms, to amplifying the voices of disabled people, and ultimately to challenging the cis-, hetero-, trans- and repronormativities, which impact all of our lives.

Kori's Reflection

Like A.J., when I first knew that I was not a woman, the words and identities that would later feel like home were, at the time, not within my scope. I identified as genderqueer and genderfuck, approaching medical transition cautiously but with desperation. The first trans men I met were performing a masculinity that was an over compensatory replication of the most toxic masculinity. Although I felt that changing my body physically was a direction I needed to explore, I made a commitment to myself before that first shot. I promised myself that accessing any privileges I may become assumed to deserve through a white male appearance would be used to hold the door open. I saw trans men in my community turning their back on non-binary or nonpassing friends and community; I committed to myself that no matter how binary I might at any point present, I wouldn't look down on or think less of those who didn't, couldn't, or wouldn't.

A couple of years after starting hormones, I was under investigation for a genetic condition that involved an appointment with a genetic counsellor, discussing the risks and alternatives to biological reproduction. At this point, I had already signed consent forms, acknowledging that my transition may have impacts on my fertility. I wasn't holding onto a future where I would biologically reproduce; this was around the same time as Thomas Beatie's first public pregnancy—he gave birth to his first child in June of 2008—and the idea of trans masculine pregnancy was just starting to tease the collective consciousness. At this point, being told that I couldn't or shouldn't use my body to breed activated a "don't tell me what to do" attitude that pushed me to seek confirmation, and eventually retraction, of that diagnosis. I started the process of many years of pausing medical transition, negotiating sperm donations, attempting to inseminate, miscarriage, apprentice parenting the children of friends and lovers, and eventually becoming pregnant and giving birth in 2016.

The trans pregnancy community I found online through the years of trying to conceive, miscarriage, pregnancy, and new parenting was a life saver. I was one of the first six people in a rudimentary Google chat where we conceived of what became Birthing and Breast or Chest Feeding for Trans Folks and Their Allies or "the big group." Over the years, as my own process went through its cycles, I stepped in and out of moderation of this group, watching it grow to over five thousand members. As the group grew bigger, more niche needs became apparent. When there were six of us, the differences of urban/rural, white/POC, partnered/solo, binary/non-binary, and pregnant people/ service providers were present but not on the front of our focus. We were mostly grateful for any connection and solidarity that we could find. As our numbers grew, the ability (and need) to further refine our affinity groups grew, too. At the time of writing this introduction, there are now countless groups, some for specific identities, others organized to support specific points in the process, whether trying to conceive, currently pregnant, grieving loss, or infant feeding. The landscape of peer support has changed dramatically over the past ten years, but much of this has happened behind closed doors in closed groups and private chat threads.

During my pregnancy, I worked with my friend and unregistered birth keeper, Amanda Phoenix, for prenatal care. She did all she could to find appropriate resources to support me, but we both found the rigid binaries and cissexist assumptions in the majority of the birth literature challenging. Books, videos, and online tools all felt not for me in their "women, mothers, mama, divine feminine" takes on pregnancy and childbirth. Amanda reached out to Esla Asher, who was also working in full spectrum doula care at the time and who had another non-binary client. The two of them reached out to their teachers, asking on behalf of their non-binary and trans clients for pregnancy and birth resources beyond the binary. Their teachers humbly told them that they needed to become the resources that they were seeking—that it was time for them to step into their position as teachers. Elsa and Amanda started hosting webinar sessions for birth workers to help improve capacity of service providers, and once I had given birth, I joined the team. We worked together to create and curate the resources we originally sought and did not find, including a six-week childbirth education course we were able to sell through our website, birthingbeyondthebinary.com. When we needed to step away from this work, we were able to hand off the website and the labour of this education to king yaa, a Black, non-binary educator, who has since taken the project further by integrating decolonized and intersectional considerations throughout.

I met A.J. as a participant in their research, which I was honoured to participate in. I had a lot to say about my own experiences as a non-binary gestational parent and wanted to see my experiences, and those of even less heard voices, make their way to the textbooks and lecture halls, preparing upcoming cohorts of doctors, nurses, lawyers, policy writers, social workers, and others who are supposed to be able to support reproduction, reproductive health, and family creation. As an outsider to academia, my own ability to do that felt limited to the position of subject, which while limited and at times problematic felt well held by A.J.'s insider/outsider non-binary academic approach. Although I have always been writing, I never saw how the jump from blog posts, short magazine articles, and peer education resources to a full printed bound book would happen. Especially once parenting— which over the first three years has involved partner separations, fleeing violence, cross-province relocation, housing insecurity, mental health crises, life threatening allergies and now a global pandemic— the idea of having a book on the go has seemed like a pie in the sky. I have been grateful to work with A.J. as they have been accommodating and supportive of the challenges I have faced in this project, always reminding me that my participation, however limited it has needed to be, was valuable.

It has been a privilege and honour to first read these chapters and to work with the authors while refining them. Having these words in print changes the landscape, making the politically personal public. I want to thank both the writers, and you, the reader, for participating in the vulnerability of this paradigm-changing work.

Joint Reflection

What magic occurs in the liminal, in-between space? What emerges from the chrysalis, after the period of transformation and renewal? What possibilities do we see for a beyond-the-binary future having worked tirelessly on this collection for over two years? Oh, dear reader, the list feels endless, rich with possibility and hope, even with the odds seemingly stacked against us. We imagine a world where trans and non-binary people can reproduce and parent without restriction—legal, political, or otherwise. We imagine a future where the harms of binary oppositions are but a distant memory and where all people can just be without having first internalized messages that differentiate the so-called right ways of being from the so-called wrong ones. We dream of a future where the state is stripped of its powers to certify the sexes and genders of its citizens, whether neonates or adults, where that certification is necessarily violent, racist, cisnormative, and hetero-sexist. Indeed, we dream of a future where the state is stripped of all of its powers, yielded so violently against so many. We look forward to social movements and activist efforts that are necessarily inter-sectional—where reproductive justice is understood as deeply and necessarily connected to decolonization, the eradication of racist capitalism, prison abolition, securing dignity and safety for sex workers, and addressing and dismantling cisheteropatriarchy.

We see this collection as an intervention on the bioessentialism that affixes certain genders to certain bodies and, by extension, certain reproductive capacities and parenting roles. It is no longer acceptable to suggest that only cisgender women can be mothers or that fatherhood is limited to cisgender men. It is no longer acceptable to violently force intersex people into sexed boxes. It is no longer acceptable for trans and non-binary people to be an afterthought—either reactionarily accommodated after the fact or tacked onto research, policy, or practice that otherwise remains unchanged. Indeed, these things have never been acceptable, and this collection is but one important contribution that interrogates the pervasive cisnormativity of reproduction and parenting practices, research, and scholarship. We are dissatisfied with efforts to reform a broken system. We are anarchist abolitionists at heart. We do not want our queer and trans families, BIPOC families, and disabled families to be simply inserted into institutions that will cause them harm. We want to reimagine a world where mutual care, community, coalition, self-determination, and autonomy are core principles. A lot of pressure to put on a wee book, we are aware. But we are hopeful that this book will create a ripple, which will be added to the ripples created by others' efforts, which will grow to a wave and then swell into a revolution.

Glossary

Androcentrism – A practice of privileging, centering or emphasizing masculine points of view, as well as masculine interests and traits; the perpetuation of a male and/or masculine world view; a practice of culturally marginalizing femininity.

Cisgender – A descriptive adjective that refers to a person whose sex assignment at birth and current gender identity align according to contemporary sociocultural values, e.g. a person who was assigned male at birth and who identifies as a man could be described as a cisgender man.

Cisnormativity – Three interconnected assumptions which are embedded into many Western colonial systems and structures; first, that there are only two sex-assignments (namely male and female, which ignores intersex people); second, that there are only two gender identity options (namely man and woman, which ignores non-binary people); third, that sex and gender are meant to align in particular ways, which are then naturalized and normalized. Under cis-normativity, it is assumed that all people ought to be cisgender, where trans people are framed as exceptional, unexpected, unnatural.

Heteronormative – The dominant and pervasive belief that hetero-sexuality is normal, natural and the preferred sexual orientation; predicated on cisnormativity and reliant on a binary understanding of gender; positions heterosexual, so-called opposite sex parents raising heterosexual children as the most viable family formation.

Heteropatriarchy – A sociopolitical system which positions cisgender, heterosexual men as having authority over all others including cis-gender women, queer and trans people who are consequently dis-empowered and disadvantaged; a colonial construct that naturalizes not only cisgender, heterosexual domination, but also white supremacy and settler colonialism.

Heterosexism – A system of discrimination, prejudice, biases, attitudes which are based on the presumption that heterosexual or so-called opposite sex attractions and relationships are natural, normal and therefore superior to other kinds of relationships.

Homonormativity – A system which privileges some gay, lesbian, bisexual people as superior to others, based on their proximity to white-centric heteropatriachy; encourages assimilation of gay, lesbian and bisexual people into conventional heterosexual institutions and norms.

Homophobia – A range of negative attitudes, prejudices, feelings, fears and aversion to gay and lesbian people, who may be used to describe intolerance to bisexual and trans people as well (but where biphobia and transphobia are more specific terms to describe these negative attitudes as they relate to these specific populations; manifests itself in interpersonal conflict and violence, legal restrictions and criminalization; hate speech, etc.

Intersectionality – A theoretical framework developed by Kimberlé Crenshaw to describe how race, gender, class and other individual characteristics intersect, combine and compound in order to create unique experiences and expressions of power, privilege, marginalization and prejudice; a way to take into account people's overlapping identities to understand their unique positionality in relation to systematic oppression

Ontology – The philosophical study of the nature of reality; involves consideration of concepts such as being, becoming, reality, existence, etc.

Transphobia – A range of negative attitudes, prejudices, feelings, fears and aversion to transgender, transsexual, non-binary and other gender diverse and gender non-conforming people; manifests itself in interpersonal conflict and violence; legal restrictions; hate speech, etc.

Notes on Contributors

Kamee Abrahamian Kamee is a supreme hyphenate who arrives in the world today as an interdisciplinary writer-artist-producer-performer-organizer and a non-binary, queer-feminist caregiver. They grew up in an immigrant suburb of Toronto and were born into an Armenian family displaced from the SWANA region. Kamee's work is steeped with relational and generative practices oriented towards ancestral reclamation, visionary fiction, and diasporic futurism. They hold a BFA/BA in film and political science (Concordia University), an MA in expressive art therapy (European Graduate Institute), and a MA/PhD in community, liberation, indigenous and eco psychologies (Pacifica Graduate Institute). Their most recent research explored legacies of relational ontologies and ethics of care by diasporic-SWANA women & queers. They've published plays, literary and academic writing, while organizing and presenting films, artwork, staged performances and workshops internationally. Kamee currently works at a global feminist movement-support organization (AWID), and they collaborate with various collectives/ad-hoc groups (HyePhen Magazine, Armenian Creatives, SWANA Ancestral Hub, Dragomanserai).

Taqdir (Taq) Kaur Bhandal ਤਕਦੀਰ ਕੌਰ ਭੰਡਾਲ is the CEO of Mahwari Research Institute, founder of IM With Periods (@imwithperiods), and author of *Self-Care Down There: An All Genders Guide to Vaginal Wellbeing*. She teaches and writes about the four seasons of menstrual/mahwari cycles, pelvic wellness, and overall health. She's also a dog lady, passionate about nachos, and nach (dance), who lives in Vancouver/Coast Salish Lands and Halifax/Mi'kmaw Treaty Territory.

Serena Lukas Bhandar is a transfemme writer, educator, and witch of Punjabi Sikh and Welsh ancestry based in Lekwungen and WSÁNEĆ territories. She is currently crafting a hybrid collection of poetry and prose, a few novels, and various other writing and plans. Find more of her writing at serenabhandar.com.

Milo Chesnut is a queer and non-binary educator, researcher, and curriculum designer. They received a Research Excellence Award from the University of Strathclyde for a PhD in trans and non-binary inclusive education. Their qualitative research focuses on "theyby" parenting. Previously, Chesnut taught high school in New York City. They organized for LGBTQ inclusion, specifically the implementation of school-wide curriculum and best practices on pronoun sharing. Their curriculum was featured in the book *Safe Is Not Enough: Better Schools for LGBTQ Students*, and their lesson plans were published in the forthcoming edited collection, *Teaching About Gender Diversity: Teacher-Tested Lesson Plans for K-12 Classrooms*. You can find out more about their work at milochesnut.com.

Eitan Codish is an Israeli American poet, social worker, and school counsellor. His poems have appeared in *Epicenter*, *Nimrod*, *Storie*, and others, both in the U.S. and abroad. His first chapbook, *Lovers and Other Still Creatures*, is available from First Matter Press. He resides in Portland, Oregon.

H. Kori Doty is a settler of European ancestry living in Lekwungen Territory after six transformative years living and learning while homesteading in Sinixt Territory. They are a community educator and their initiatives in sexual health, harm reduction, trans resilience building, and practical skills have been driven by a hunger for justice and equity. They are a solo parent to a three-year-old; from this position, they have challenged the province to change the way babies are assigned gender. They are a leader in best practices in education and strive to change hearts, minds, relationships, systems, and paradigms with their patience, eloquence, and perspectives.

Jan E. Estrellado is a queer, genderqueer, and trans-masculine Filipinx parent. Jan is an assistant professor at Alliant International University, San Diego, and a licensed psychologist whose research and clinical interests focus broadly on trauma psychology, multicultural psychology, and social justice as well as issues related to training and supervision.

Olivia Fischer is a queer, non-binary, childless settler who lives, studies, and works on the unceded territories of the Coast Salish people. They completed their MA in counselling psychology at UBC and focused their thesis research on the birth stories of non-binary people. Actively engaged in this work, they are committed to elevating the voices of marginalized people and resisting negative hetero-normative, transphobic cultural beliefs and messages. In addition, they research sexuality in both the transgender and cancer world. For work, Olivia coordinates and facilitates workshops focused on preventing and responding to intimate partner violence within queer and trans communities.

Viridian Fen is a queer trans non-binary author, a multimedia visual artist, and a nationally certified ASL/English interpreter. Through a dedicated practice of self-parenting with a variety of professional support, Viridian recovered from growing up in a Christian funda-mentalist environment and has been growing into an expansive, expressive person. They have been a partnered parent for almost nine years and have put down roots in Chattanooga, Tennessee.

A.J. Lowik has a PhD from the Institute for Gender, Race, Sexuality and Social Justice at the University of British Columbia, where their research focuses on trans people's reproductive lives and health. A.J. has worked extensively with abortion providers and other reproductive health providers on creating trans-inclusive policies, practices, and spaces. They are the Gender Equity Advisor with the Centre for Gender and Sexual Health Equity, where their work focuses on addressing the erasure of trans and non-binary people in research, healthcare service provision, and medical education. A.J. loves cats, yoga, board games, and potato chips. They are an unapologetic feminist, a queer lib-erationist, and work to disrupt cisnormativity everywhere they go. You can find out more about their work at ajlowik.com.

Alanna Aiko Moore is a queer, mixed-race Asian Pacific Islander parent and the sociology, ethnic, and gender studies librarian at the UC San Diego. Alanna's research interests include intersectionality, queerness, mentoring, activism, and issues affecting women of colour librarians. She has also served as a director and organizer at social justice community organizations.

Sunny Nestler lives on unceded Coast Salish territory / Vancouver BC. Nestler received an MFA from Emily Carr University of Art and Design in 2013, where they currently teach drawing and natural science. Nestler has published work as an illustrator and book/zine maker and exhibited in North America. Nestler's work is based in drawing and studies mechanisms of biological life using a process that mimics DNA replication and mutation. Their work is multidisciplinary and includes video, installation, performance, and painting. Their subject matter cross pollinates biological processes, DIY communities, and unusual landscapes with the political affect of relatedness and mutation.

Pidgeon Pagonis is an intersex activist, writer, artist, speaker, and consultant. They are the cofounder of the Intersex Justice Project, have produced informational videos that centre intersex voices, and were honored as a LGBT Champion of Change in 2015 by the Obama White House. You can find out more about their work at http://pid.ge.

Moira Pérez earned her PhD in philosophy at the University of Buenos Aires, Argentina, where she is currently assistant professor at the Department of Philosophy. She is a researcher at the National Scientific and Technical Research Council (CONICET), specializing in violence and identity, particularly institutional and epistemic violence towards political minorities. Her work has been published in compilations in Argentina and abroad as well as in the *Journal of Homosexuality* (USA), *Lambda Nordica* (Sweden), *InterAlia* (Poland), and *Estudos Feministas* (Brazil), among others.

Blas Radi is a philosophy professor at the University of Buenos Aires, where he teaches theory of knowledge and feminist philosophy. His work combines philosophical research with human rights activism, particularly in relation to the trans* community. Currently, he is the coordinator of the Independent Chair of Trans* Studies at the School of Philosophy and Literature (UBA). Blas is currently pursuing his PhD in philosophy at the University of Buenos Aires, thanks to a doctoral scholarship awarded by CONICET (National Scientific and Technical Research Council).

Saige Whesch hails at heart from the tropics of Larrakia country in the Top End, where they repeated their final year of high school and part of a creative industries degree undiagnosed. Saige is a Nonbinary and dynamically disabled, neurodivergent Queer working as a consultant, performer, videographer, author, sometimes activist, constant proud parent and primary partner. They live on unceded Ngunnawal, Ngambri and Ngurmal lands. Debuting in this book, Saige seeks to impart supportive tactics and empower the noesis of questioning internal and systemic structures. You can find Saige on Instagram @TheStoryOfSai doing more of whatever happens next.

Deepest appreciation to
Demeter's monthly Donors

DEMETER

Daughters
Rebecca Bromwich
Summer Cunningham
Tatjana Takseva
Debbie Byrd
Fiona Green
Tanya Cassidy
Vicki Noble
Bridget Boland
Naomi McPherson
Myrel Chernick

Sisters
Amber Kinser
Nicole Willey
Christine Peets